Chris Mercurio

NEW PATRIOT PUBLISHING

Copyright © 2011 by Chris Mercurio
All rights reserved.

NEW PATRIOT PUBLISHING

www.newpatriotpublishing.com

All rights reserved. No part of this publication may be reproduced, stored in a retrieval system, or transmitted, in any form or by any means, electronic, mechanical, photo copying, recording, or otherwise, without the written prior permission of New Patriot Publishing LLC.

Paperback Edition
ISBN – 0-9828885-8-9
ISBN – 978-0-9828885-8-2

Electronic Editions (Ebook)
ISBN – 0-9828885-7-0
ISBN – 978-0-9828885-7-5

Printed in the United States of America.

To my two boys, may you dream big and always be guided by the Truth. Also, to my wife Stacy who inspires me every day to be a better man.

DEAR OBAMA

Acknowledgements:

I would like to thank my parents for their gift of humor and unwavering love and support. I would also like to recognize Granddad and Papa for their years of service to this country and for exemplifying those of the "Greatest Generation." Finally, I would like to thank all the friends and family who supported me along the way in this endeavor. It meant a great deal to me.

About the Author:

He likes ESPN and In-N-Out Burger.

DEAR OBAMA

DEAR OBAMA

This work is fictional.... except for the parts that are true.

DEAR OBAMA

DEAR OBAMA

DEAR OBAMA

DEAR OBAMA

"The biggest argument against democracy is to have a five minute conversation with the average voter."

– Winston Churchill

DEAR OBAMA

DEAR OBAMA

Introduction

Like most Americans, I will always remember where I was when Barack Obama was declared the 44th President of the United States of America. I was in my five-year-old son's bedroom holding a waste bucket for him as he vomited uncontrollably. Conventional wisdom would have you believe that he came down with the same flu bug that afflicted his little brother just a few hours before. But one might make the case that he was giving us a glimpse of the near future. I cannot accept or deny that theory, although it does seem ironic that my two-year-old began vomiting right about the time that the exit polls were released.

A conservative friend of mine had a contingency plan should Obama win. On November 5th, the day after the election, he would implement the plan: a daily regimen of Wild Turkey, Quaaludes and the music of Simon & Garfunkel. His only "hope" was to remain barely conscious throughout an Obama presidency. As a political moderate, I found it a bit extreme and scoffed at his idea, but at least he never threatened to move to Alec Baldwinia if Obama won the election.

It's not surprising that the American people took to Barack Obama. After all, he is one of us. For two years he had us glued to our TVs. We listened as his words of truth soared above the teleprompter, words that inspired an entire generation of text messengers. America is grateful to Obama for having awakened this critical voting bloc. We couldn't be more fortunate than to have the future of this nation resting in the hands of those obsessed with MTV and

DEAR OBAMA

Sony PlayStation. I'm certain our Founders would be equally impressed with their skills in Madden NFL Football.

Although I was initially hesitant to embrace the euphoria that surrounded candidate Obama, I feel it is now time to join in the enthusiasm. I know he's not in the Oval Office yet, but Barack Obama is the best President this country has ever had.

DEAR OBAMA

"My friends, we live in the greatest nation in the history of the world. I hope you'll join with me as we try to change it."

– Presidential hopeful Barack Obama, June 7, 2008

November 5, 2008

Dear Obama,

Let me officially congratulate you on a most impressive and timely Election Day win. Thankfully, the country wanted "change," and that's what your campaign delivered in an overwhelming fashion. No longer will the citizens of this country suffer under George W. Bush and be held hostage by a president so hell-bent on keeping this nation and its people safe. The days of cowboy diplomacy are over and the days of Neville Chamberlain are here again! We are proud to have your back, Mr. President-elect, as you march around the world and firmly tell our enemies we're sorry for any misunderstandings.

    Because of the historic nature of this election, I feel compelled to document your presidency. You have already given so much to this country and since I am unable to name a school or street after you, words will be my way of honoring you. Let's call this a political diary, a journal of your "phatness." If it is okay with you, I'll simply address you as "Dear Obama."

Sincerely,
Chris

DEAR OBAMA

November 8, 2008

Dear Obama,

I must be honest and say that I don't know much about Marxism other than a few catch phrases such as "redistribution of wealth," "class warfare" and "change we can believe in." I thought history had proven Marxism to be an utter failure, so I never had much interest. But now it seems to be gaining momentum and generating an enthusiasm not seen in this country since the Carter years.

Your friends and colleagues such as the mild-mannered "Reverend" Wright, your first mentor Frank Marshall Davis, Windy City pal and aspiring Caponian, Mike Klonsky, and the always-lovable terrorist/professor Bill Ayers must be encouraged to see that radicalism is not only again in vogue but is a prerequisite for cabinet positions or prestigious appointments in academia. Considering all this, I feel it is my duty as an American to study and adopt this political ideology while doing my best to fight against the exploitation of the workingman. My only question—where do I begin?

I first googled Marxism to see if there were any online application forms. I also printed out forms for Communism and Socialism, just to make sure I didn't put all my eggs in one basket. Socialism is my safety ideology in case I don't get into either of my top two choices. Unfortunately, the process is a little different than signing-up for a YMCA membership. There are no EZ registration forms. It isn't as simple as giving my name, address and DOB. Marxism is more about theory and philosophy. It is plain to see that if I am going to have any success at all, I will have to reeducate myself using self-enforced repression and indoctrination. I guess I had better begin with the basics.

Lesson #1—the definition of Marxism:

> The notion of economic determination—that political and social structures are determined by the economic conditions of people. Marxism calls for a classless society where all means of production are commonly owned, a system to be reached as an inevitable result of the struggle between capitalists and workers.

If only Madison and Adams had been fortunate enough to attend any one of our current university programs, we wouldn't be left with this aging system mired with freedoms and opportunity. Although I used to admire them, maybe their little experiment has run its course. We are long overdue for a new direction, or it is, to quote you Mr. President-elect, "time to fundamentally transform the United States of America."

As I continued my research, I came across an online class offered by the ACLU. It isn't accredited, but the units are recognized by the Ivy League and are internationally transferable. The curriculum is geared towards beginners and focuses on the basic tenants such as oppression, exploitation, and Ruth Bader Ginsburg. It appeared to have everything I was looking for, yet as I glanced over the course syllabus, I was disappointed to see that it didn't include some of the more important thinkers such as Engels, Lenin, and Maher. Though I decided not to enroll, I still got the free coffee mug just for showing interest in the class.

It is engraved with a quote from the founder of the ACLU, Roger Baldwin: "We are for socialism, disarmament, and ultimately for the abolition of the state itself." What a way to start the morning! Just think had I actually signed up for the course I could have received the complete set of commemorative Keith Olbermann dinner plates.

Maybe another time . . .

Sincerely,
Chris

November 13, 2008

Dear Obama,

I was watching CNN last night and Jack Cafferty happened to be talking about "Joe the Plumber" and what role he had, if any, in the campaign. He went on to show the now famous clip of you explaining to Joe how you didn't want to penalize his success, but "share the wealth" with the guy behind him. I thought I sympathized with Joe because he appeared to be just like me: middle class, raising a family, worried about taxes, just your "Average Joe." As I watched, I realized that the most important connection I have with Joe is that we are both bald men, a neglected voting bloc consisting of millions of tax-paying Americans.

For the first time I thought, "I am a 37-year-old bald

man, and frankly, I don't think it's *fair*." Why should other men have ample amounts of hair while I struggle every day to keep alive any existing remnants? You promised a new computer to every child in this country, you promised everyone health coverage, you promised every Irish-American folk dancer handmade wooden clogs, well I want a promise that every bald American is going to have hair. I want you to walk up to a man with a full head of hair and say, "I don't want to penalize your scalp; I just want to share your hair with the bald guy behind you." That is the kind of country I want to live in, one that represents the disenfranchised, and one that will finally stand up and say, "Equality for all!"

    I realize I'm venturing into uncharted waters. The bald constituency has never been well represented in Washington. Then again, Washington has never seen a President like you before—someone who sticks up for the little guy and has the resume to prove it. You're the kind of action-taker that will ultimately help people like me, the bald and less fortunate. For example, you once headed the Chicago Annenberg Challenge, a school reform project intended to "help educate children that are less fortunate." Surprisingly, the project failed and the schools never saw a dime of the pledged $50 million (to this day that money is still unaccounted for). But that doesn't take away from the fact that you and fellow board member Bill Ayers fought tooth and nail to help educate (radicalize) these school children through traditional (revolutionary) means of teaching (indoctrination).

DEAR OBAMA

If that's not change I can believe in, then I have no idea what is.

Sincerely,
Chris

November 19, 2008

Dear Obama,

My last entry got me thinking and I've come up with a Bald Plan. Like all grassroots campaigns, it will start at the local level and will recruit as many bald volunteers as possible. Getting the word out to the community will be vital. To accomplish this we will need to gather signatures for petitions, have weekly house meetings, contact our local media, and raise money from various donors. Funding will particularly help my "Bald Awareness" marketing blitz.

Our campaign plans to strategically place posters of Dr. Phil and Dennis Franz around town for maximum impact. I may be getting a little ahead of myself, but I'm counting on them for support. We will also display posters of Vice President-elect Joe Biden warning people of the dangers of hair plugs. Granted it's a common procedure, but if the plugs are inserted too deeply into the scalp varying side effects will result. The most prevalent symptoms in Mr. Biden's case appear to be confusion, irritability, and an odd behavioral resemblance to Inspector Clouseau.

At some point, I'm sure I'll be tempted to employ the tactics of legendary Chicago community agitator, Saul

DEAR OBAMA

Alinsky. It's no wonder that you were greatly influenced by the model set forth in his book, *Rules for Radicals*. Under the tutelage of John L. McKnight, a Northwestern University professor and direct disciple of Alinsky, you said you gained "the best education I ever had." Sadly, this comment provoked an immediate firestorm at your alma maters Columbia and Harvard. Alumni bewildered and seeking an explanation accused certain faculty members of pro-American bias in the classroom.

Of course, this is all wishful thinking. I have to understand that I'm still wet behind the ears when it comes to activism and thuggery, so it might take me a little while to get a handle on community organizing and the Alinsky model. If all goes well, I hope to get my grassroots campaign off the ground in the second half of 2009.

Sincerely,
Chris

November 21, 2008

Dear Obama,

I've drafted a bill to submit to our local congressman titled, "The Follicle Stimulus Package." The ultimate goal is to gather the support and sponsorship needed to send this all the way to Capitol Hill. If we're successful in getting this passed, qualified citizens, who will be required to show proof of baldness, will receive a hair restoration kit from the federal government. This will consist of assorted creams, stimulants, and traditional minoxidils (Rogaine). To those opting for an alternative method, herbal remedies such as the popular Upper Eastside concoction of Indian gooseberry, coconut oil, and paprika may be considered.

Sadly, we know the statistics of revitalizing follicle growth. To say it's very difficult would be an understatement. With this in mind, a secondary piece of legislation would be introduced. The "Hair Redistribution Act of 2010" will piggyback the stimulus package as a pledge to those who suffer from severe cases of alopecia. Thunder dome may erupt on the Senate floor due to the extreme or even radical aspects of this measure. However, I would expect it to pass considering most in the room would benefit from this legislation.

The basic idea of the bill is simple: the transfer of a portion of hair from an affluent follicle source to a desolate region on the scalp of a deserving Baldletariat. The most controversial part of the plan would be for those that resist voluntary hair extraction. In such cases "forceful hair removal" will be required and enforced by local youths with blond hair, blue eyes, and brown shirts.

Public perception may be negative in the beginning, but there is plenty of excess hair to go around. We've all seen the disturbing images of mullets and would have to agree that a few snips in the back would not only help maintain adequate inventory levels, but would help restore family values.

I take heart knowing that you, President-elect Obama, will be a champion of my proposals. I say this because you are a fair man, a man who has battled his own adversity growing up. I can't help but admire you for having the courage to endure private school in Hawaii for all those years. It obviously instilled a toughness in you that helped get you through your time at Columbia and Harvard. One can only wonder where you found the resolve to make it to Lakeshore Drive in Chicago. What horrors you must have encountered as you bounced around the political scene in Lincoln Park and Michigan Avenue night after night discussing kitchen table issues and racketeering methods with the honorable Mayor Daly and his cronies.

Sincerely,
Chris

November 25, 2008

Dear Obama,

I'm concerned about Joe Biden. He has been MIA since the upturn in his erratic behavior. I recently watched a YouTube video of him singing "Margaritaville" at a karaoke lounge in Boca Raton. However, I do question its authenticity since the picture was out of focus.

Sincerely worried,
Chris

DEAR OBAMA

November 28, 2008

Dear Obama,

I apologize that my last entry had to be so serious. Unfortunately, my fears regarding Mr. Biden's mental health have never been greater. In fact, I am now convinced that the administration desperately needs a cerebral warning system. I have taken the liberty to design a system that will track Mr. Biden's daily coherency. I modeled it after the Department of Homeland Security's terrorism threat-level color code. My prototype for this gauge has a built in LED barometer display ranging from "Pauly Shore" to "Cousin Eddie." "Cousin Eddie" is obviously the desired and optimal level. I'll be sending it to you soon.

Sincerely,
Chris

November 29, 2008

Dear Obama,

I find it very exciting that "patriotic" Americans who used to mock the Oval Office out of embarrassment and disgust can now beam with pride as you finally return respect and dignity to the presidency. Who wouldn't be proud of a fist-bumping, Jay-Z- listening and backward-baseball-cap-wearing leader of the free world? It is all way too cool. I guess you're kind of like the Ashton Kutcher of presidents, which in most spring break locations is an incredible honor.

DEAR OBAMA

Actually, it probably wouldn't hurt to team up with Ashton for some good old hilarious comedy. What you should do when you take office is schedule a special address to the country and say, "Based on the current economic conditions, my administration has decided we will go back to the country's original form of government, including lower taxes, limited power, adherence to the constitution, and minimal criminal appointees." After a few minutes of trying to be serious, Ashton, wearing an Uncle Sam costume, could jump out from behind one of those Greek columns. Then the two of you could look straight into the camera and say, "America ... you've just been punk'd!"

Sincerely,
Chris

November 30, 2008

Dear Obama,

As expected, you've done a fantastic job with your cabinet appointments thus far. I disagree with the criticism you've received regarding all of the ex-Clintonites. If it weren't for those pesky confirmation hearings, your administration could be stacked with all of your past associates. As it stands now, it looks like 70% of your appointees are from the Clinton administration. Not bad for "change we can believe in."

I was a little surprised by your pick for Chief of Staff,

DEAR OBAMA

Rahm Emanuel. I only say this because I picked your friend and former PLO advisor, Rashid Khalidi in my political fantasy league. My analysis ranked Khalidi first. Second, I had supporter and anti-Semite veteran, Lewis Farrakhan and third, I picked Joy Behar—for obvious reasons.

I would be lying if I said that I wasn't a little disappointed you didn't appoint Mr. Khalidi. I must have put too much emphasis on the fact that his wife was once a translator for Yasser Arafat. I still have hope that you will find a position in your cabinet for him and your buddy Billy Ayers. It would be like the good old days when you all hung out together as professors in Chicago. "The Three Racketeers" together again in Washington—what a headline!

Now don't get me wrong, I think Rahm Emanuel is a solid choice for Chief of Staff. I like the fact that he has always been a supporter of Israel. I think this bodes well for your credibility. It may cause a few problems should your proposed potluck dinner with Hamas occur, but all will be forgotten if Rahm brings that potato salad I've heard so much about. I was surprised and somewhat intrigued to learn he is an accomplished ballet dancer. It's refreshing to see politicians who have talents other than undermining the American people. I'm not sure many people know that Condoleezza Rice is a trained classical pianist, or that she was the youngest Provost in Stanford's history. Even Barney Frank is venturing outside of Washington, as he is currently negotiating a contract with Audio Books.

Sincerely,
Chris

DEAR OBAMA

December 1, 2008

Dear Obama,

I have had only one concern up until this point, what was all this talk about you being a Centrist? You had me all confused, that is, until you appointed Eric Holder as your Attorney General. How ingenious, Machiavellian, or should I say Axelrodian. No offense, Mr. President-elect, but that move has the post-moralist written all over it. Only your campaign manager could have orchestrated this scheme—using the others as a smokescreen to sneak in Holder—brilliant! Keeping Gates and appointing Jim Jones and Larry Summers to your administration will be more than enough political capital to get Holder confirmed. Of course, we'll hear all about the Marc Rich and the FALN terrorists' pardons, but I have six words for Mr. Holder: "I have no recollection of that."

Holder's appointment reinforces my confidence that your plan is to change this country through judicial appointments, not just the Federal Supreme Court, but also the lower appellate courts. That's where you can really gut this country—in a good way, of course. I trust you're going to use California's 9th Circuit of Appeals as your court model. Living in California, I can vouch for its commitment to the Constitution. Initially, I was concerned about some of its decisions. Looking back, I see how I mistook sound judicial intent for complete lunacy and grounds for disbarment. I realize now that swindlers with law degrees know better than the will of the people. It's reassuring to know that the good folks in black robes are there to keep us (the people) in line when our thinking gets a little wacky.

I can't stress it enough. Look to California, Mr. Former-Community-Organizer-Turned-President. The progressives are doing great work out here on the Left Coast. They have finally taken control and have us on a direct path to Europe, at least the Europe of decades ago. It might seem a little regressive when you look at it from the outside, but the model works. Don't let the recent conservative elections in Italy, France, Germany, Poland, Czech Republic, Hungary, and Slovakia fool you.

In closing, I would just like to say, "Job well done." According to my analysis, you've done the best job so far of any President-elect in the first 23 days and 48 seconds following an election.

Sincerely,
Chris

December 3, 2008

Dear Obama,

I'm in the process of putting the final touches on a fundraising grant proposal specifically for Tinseltown. Getting Hollywood to support the cause would help tremendously. I will share more once it's completed, but to give you an idea, it discusses the recent persecution of bald Tibetans, and how hair poachers are becoming more prevalent in certain areas. The black market for hair has skyrocketed recently with people paying top dollar.

As a man of action, I think you would be proud that I've already begun distributing my volunteer flyers. I'm not one for self-adulation, but I have to admit they came out pretty darn good. With any luck, this will be the first step in a crucial and long-lasting movement.

Here is a sample:

****

BALD VOLUNTEERS WANTED

- Looking for highly motivated individuals suffering from hair depletion or sympathetic to the plight.
- Duties include: handing out pamphlets, telemarketing, community organizing, and purging those opposed to the ideology of the Bald Race (Alopecia eugenics).
- Operating under the code name "Schutzstaffel" or "Friendly Hair Admirers."
- Paramilitary, Union, and ACORN experience preferred.
- If you are interested or have questions please call Chris at **1-888-NO-BALF-1**

****

What do you think? Obviously, I wish I had caught the mistake on the 888 number, but oh well. I confess that the general premise of my plan is based on your idea of a Civilian Police Force. I don't know about you, but I have no intention of targeting homeschoolers, conservative advocacy groups, or political dissidents—at least not at first. In the future, I would not hesitate to merge with your Civilian Police Force if you needed my assistance.

I've also been doing some research on how Global Balding is surprisingly just as responsible for the planet in peril as man-made global warming. Until now, the scientific community has been apathetic, if not a little stubborn, in accepting this theory as a viable cause. In my analysis, I go into great detail explaining how the earth is actually going bald and how eco-discrimination is keeping scientists from disseminating the truth. Deforestation, or man-made balding, is at the heart of my thesis and the main culprit of this unprecedented environmental civil rights issue.

Unfortunately, my work is not as glamorous as others, which will make it difficult to gain Hollywood's support. I am hopeful they will consider my proposal once they've seen the recent satellite images of earth and how it's starting to look more and more like Larry David.

Keep your fingers crossed . . .

Sincerely,
Chris

DEAR OBAMA

December 5, 2008

Dear Obama,

It must get tiresome listening to the naysayers' incessant nagging about your foreign policy inexperience. You haven't even taken office and already they say you're a complete failure. What they don't seem to understand is that you are at a disadvantage. How can your critics expect you to conduct an effective foreign policy when none of the other world leaders are on Facebook?

I hear Putin is fond of tweeting, but seriously ...

Sincerely,
Chris

December 9, 2008

Dear Obama,

Rod Blagojevich! I can't find a TV channel, radio station, or internet site without hearing or seeing this guy's name. You must have been shocked when you heard the news. Naturally, people like Hannity and Rush are playing the guilt by association game. How many times do we have to hear how for twenty years you sat in the pews of Rev. Wright's church, or about shady land deals with the slumlord Tony Rezko, or how you spent time professionally and socially with the unrepentant terrorist

DEAR OBAMA

William Ayers? Blah, blah, blah. . .

Now they're all giddy thinking they have Blagojevich to add to the mix. I hope they don't rehash your past relationship with Blago. Who cares if you ran in the same circles, supported each other's campaigns, and socialized at dinner parties and public events? Why scrutinize your past when we the people would rather watch you shoot jump shots and flex your pectorals on the beach.

The good news is that the MSM (Mainstream Media) know you're innocent. Even though there are no real details yet, the media's intuition is usually right on the money. These pit bulls, hungry for the truth, will no doubt exhaust themselves scouring over the evidence in search of "The Real Story." I'm sure that by the end of their investigation we will know all we need to know—including your current shoe size and favorite fondue restaurant.

To me, this story is just another example of your strong character—you are the only Chicago politician ever to resist corruption. It's more than obvious you made a valiant effort to avoid all these people when you could. If ever you did see political corruption around you, you had the moral courage and leadership not to blow the whistle (let's be honest, the last thing we want for a president is a rat). Besides, whistle blowing becomes a distraction and makes people feel uncomfortable. A lot of good it did Sarah Palin in Alaska when she tried to root out corruption within her own party.

Regardless, what conservative pundits don't understand is that your intellect transcends all of this nonsense. Even if you were somehow connected, your Ivy League education alone affords you complete immunity.

DEAR OBAMA

It will be interesting to see how the story plays out . . .

Sincerely,
Chris

P.S. It's amazing how much Blagojevich looks like the guy who hooked up illegal cable for some of my friends back in college.

December 10, 2008

Dear Obama,

Please disregard my November 25th entry. I'm happy to report that Vice President-elect Biden was seen just two days ago rollerblading on the boardwalk in Venice Beach, California. Eyewitnesses said they saw him wearing a tie-dyed shirt and powder blue Dolphin shorts. He had on proper safety gear and appeared to be in excellent spirits. He briefly stopped at a street vendor and browsed through some driftwood carvings of sea life. He then adjusted his kneepads and continued on his way.

There I was, getting all worked up for nothing . . .

Sincerely relieved,
Chris

DEAR OBAMA

December 12, 2008

Dear Obama,

So it looks like the Governor was trying to sell your open Senate seat to the highest bidder. I heard Sen. Durbin (D-IL) was planning to make an offer until one of his aides reminded him that he already was a senator. I guess "Blago" even considered giving the seat to himself. Wiretaps confirm that he was "Senate candidate #5" and that he turned down his own bid because he thought he could get more money. It's just a bad situation all the way around, or like you said, "It's a very sad day for Illinois."

Apparently, he already has the support of former Illinois Governor and current inmate, George Ryan. He immediately reached out to "Hot Rod," saying there was nothing to worry about. He assured Blagojevich that it's a smooth, if not pleasant transition from the Windy City to prison. He was also quoted as saying, "I'm saddened by these accusations against the Governor; however, I must say that I'm relieved because we've been looking for months for a fourth for Bridge."

I really do sympathize with you, Mr. President-elect. You must feel helpless sitting there watching all of your old friends, "the gang," getting picked off one by one. I saw that they even subpoenaed the loan records from your real estate deal with Tony Rezko. Can't you guys buy a break– literally?

I mean, let's be honest here. Republicans are the ones who are mired in this culture of corruption. Don't think for a minute we've forgotten about Sarah Palin and The-clothes-the-RNC-provided-for-me-gate. The tentacle on this grease fire is never ending. If what I'm reading in the *Daily Kos* is true, she is going to have to come up with a darn good explanation of where her campaign scrunchies and hand-woven scarves came from. There's even word of an unreported turtleneck they "conveniently" left off the records. Now, I'm not suggesting Fitzgerald drop the Blagojevich case for this, but let's not close the door either.

I know some would look at the infidelities of John Edwards, Eliot Spitzer, and current New York Governor, David Patterson as a permanent stain against the Democratic Party. To the untrained eye, the corruption charges against William "Cold Cash" Jefferson (D-LA), or tax-dodger Charlie Rangel (D-NY), and our newest member, Governor Rod Blagojevich should be worrisome to party leaders. Even the "friends of Angelo" sweetheart mortgage rate deals that you, Kent Conrad (D-ND), and Chris Dodd (D-CT) received might be viewed as suspicious or hypocritical. Yet the keen observer can easily conclude that the person who is truly guilty is George W. Bush.

I'm not exactly sure what the connection is to W, but considering he has been responsible for so many ills in this country one must exist. We already know he is responsible for slow internet connection, gout, and Donald Trump's hair. It doesn't take a mathematical genius to figure out the probability here.

Being the stand-up man that you are, I know you will take the high road and defend your predecessor. I can appreciate that. But I have to believe that W made living in this country so unbearable the last eight years that the aforementioned honest public servants had no choice but to fall prey to corruption. Their actions were their way of protesting the policies of the outgoing President and lashing out against oppressive right-wing ideology. They should be celebrated for standing up for their convictions and expressing their indignation. When it's all said and done, the Blago case will be another failure in an already failed Bush administration.

Sincerely,
Chris

December 14, 2008

Dear Obama,

The pressure is mounting for Blagojevich to resign. Apparently the Illinois House Speaker is appointing a special committee to review the possibility of impeaching the Governor. It shouldn't come as much of a surprise. Here is the most recent official transcript of the charges against him:

- Sale of US Senate appointment
- Misuse of state funding to induce firing of *Chicago Tribune* editorial writers
- Refusing several pleas to get a haircut during tenure as governor
- Numerous pay-to-play schemes

- Implementing Chicago's version of "Don't ask, Don't tell." (This assumes all politicians are corrupt. If one suspects that a politician is honest, don't ask, if they are honest and someone inquires, don't tell.)

There are rumors that if Blagojevich is convicted he plans to use the experience as a stepping-stone to advance his political career. If for some odd reason it doesn't work out, he hopes to teach at a local university.

Sincerely,
Chris

December 17, 2008

Dear Obama,

What a surprise—you continue to rewrite history! After continued extensive analysis, I've come to the conclusion that your performance as President-elect on the 7th Wednesday after an election, but before winter solstice, is superior to any past president.

It actually turned out to be a nail-biter. President Taft gave you a good run for your money. After his grueling battle against Roosevelt, he reportedly spent his 7th Wednesday preparing a delicious Cornish game hen for a party of 30 on short notice. The only reason it was close was because I had to consider Blagogate. If it weren't for that, it would have been a blowout. Plus it turns out that Taft forgot to put out the yams until dinner was nearly over.

Sincerely,
Chris

December 18, 2008

Dear Obama,

Unfortunately, it appears that your Chief of Staff, Rahm Emanuel might be in a little more trouble than some had anticipated. It looks like he had 21 conversations with Blagojevich regarding your open Senate seat. Thankfully, the media is doing their job and not seriously looking into it. Their controlled amnesia has helped suppress any recollection of the transparency you promised during your campaign. I just hope it's enough to help Mr. Emanuel weasel out of all this. I know you don't want to lose a guy like him, especially one who views the current economic disaster as a way to push through the extreme measures of your agenda. Who can forget when he said, "You never want a serious crisis to go to waste." As much as the media are trying to exonerate Rahm, they are still doing a respectable job of reporting the facts and details— as they see it.

Sincerely,
Chris

DEAR OBAMA

December 19, 2008

Dear Obama,

Who hasn't been following the story of troubled Wall Street investor and major donor for the Democratic Party, Bernie Madoff? Major news networks have been all over it, but oddly have yet to disclose his allegiance to and financial support of the Democratic Party. His crimes include swindling billions from investors in an elaborate Ponzi scheme. In his defense, it was at least a voluntary Ponzi scheme, whereas the federal government is running a mandatory one.

On the surface, it would appear that Madoff's scam is the work of a right-winger. Unfortunately, that's not the case. However, I wouldn't rule out the possibility that Mr. Madoff was slipped one of those conservative party drugs. Similar to a Mickey and a Roofie, the "Righty" has exploded onto the political party scene. It wouldn't surprise me in the least if they found traces of this drug in his bloodstream. It wouldn't be difficult for any Fox News operative to sneak into a Democratic fundraiser for transgendered, eco-Rastafarians and slip him the drug.

Nevertheless, this circus with Mr. Madoff has brought back memories of the old Enron gang. Who could forget the footage of Ken Lay and Jeff Skilling as they were marched off to prison amidst the media frenzy? Every other minute the commentators referred to them as "Republicans Ken Lay and Jeff Skilling." In fact, the media should begin referring to Bernie as a Republican, as he was most likely scheming while under the influence of conservatism. Until we find out more, he'll just have to remain under house arrest in his Upper-East-Side-seven-million-dollar-apartment. That was a terribly harsh decision by leftist judge Lawrence M. McKenna.

This story is just one more reminder of why I respect the media so much. Their lack of agenda and desire to protect their own is commendable. This is why I hope someday to make it to Caracas for the annual World Media Expo. I don't know how or when, but I will get there, that much I vow. I would never expect to stay in the Blitzer and Gergen suites, but give me a cot, a blanket, and couple issues of *Workers' Magazine* and I'll be in heaven.

It would be a once in a lifetime opportunity to spend time with the people shaping this country's dialogue. Take the headlines from the AP article I just read: "Obama left with little time to curb global warming. Cooling trend illustrates how fast the world is warming." Seriously, who wouldn't want to spend time with these folks? I'd love to just pick their brains on subjects such as democracy, lint, and Khloe Kardashian.

Sincerely,
Chris

December 23, 2008

Dear Obama,

I was so delighted to see you and Abraham Lincoln on the cover of *Newsweek*. The Right is all bent out of shape over the cover story, but clearly they cannot deny the similarities. The most obvious, of course, being that Lincoln was the 16th President and you were born in 1961. When you switch the last two numbers it makes 16! You are also both considered to be among the best presidents of all time (the next four years should solidify that honor for you). You are both skinny and roughly the same height—give or take a few inches. You both smoke and wear cool hats. Although, I don't think he would look as good in your White Sox cap as you would in his Stovepipe. And there is no way he could pull off wearing it backwards the way you often do.

The one small exception I have to the comparison with Lincoln is that he fought for the individual, whereas you fight for bigger government. Since my political conversion, I'm starting to see how increased governmental intrusion in our lives is for the betterment of the individual. Lincoln would probably disagree with that, but in his defense, he was still a fairly raw and immature politician when he became president.

I see they're also throwing FDR's name out there. In general, I feel they're right on the money. The unmistakable comparison is when he claimed, "increasing the tax paid by individuals was the American thing to do." We all know that FDR was the first Socialist President in the US. He also happened to be a master of political rhetoric. In fact, his rhetoric was so good that he got himself elected four times in a row—a feat you could achieve with five hundred million tied behind your back.

The main point they're making is that you're taking office at a time of extreme economic uncertainty, much like

DEAR OBAMA

FDR did. He took office in 1933 following the market crash and Great Depression. After taking office, he wasted no time doubling-down on Hoover's policies, which included the beloved tax increase. Roosevelt criticized Hoover for not raising taxes high enough and then proceeded to double the corporate tax rate, impose an excise tax on dividends, a capital stock tax, and liquor taxes. The highest marginal rate reached 79% in 1936. By 1938 unemployment had only doubled to 20+%, which was far less than had it tripled. Those tax increases played a major factor in the spike in unemployment. You are one lucky dog. You couldn't have an easier or more detailed blueprint to follow.

You know, I was thinking that it would be kind of neat if *Newsweek* decided to write a series of comparisons. Each month they could have your picture with a different historical/important figure. For instance, February's issue could have you and Martin Luther King, Jr. In March, perhaps you could be on the cover with Gandhi. Maybe Jason Bourne in April (I would have said Jack Bauer, but he has no respect for the rights of terrorists). Actually, the ultimate would be two pictures of you side by side, but then again, I don't even know if you could compare to you. You could even take it a step further and go with a trinity theme—three glorious pictures of you in the form of a triangle.

I should probably stop before I get ridiculous . . .

Sincerely,
Chris

DEAR OBAMA

December 25, 2008

Dear Obama,

Merry Winter Happy Solstice Kwanza Holiday! I don't have much time to write today due to a full slate of family obligations. However, I wanted to make sure that some of the focus was on you today. Jesus has had his 2,000 plus years of fame. What do you say we give someone else a chance now? This may sound sacrilegious, but this is clearly your time. How much more evidence do the people need of your messianic complex? We've all heard the stories of those stricken with irritable bowel syndrome healed at one of your campaign rallies simply by touching the hem on your pant leg. Just look at the lines of followers waiting to see you. Fans are waiting hours and hours in the cold, rain, and snow just to catch a glimpse of you (similar to the Jonas Brothers). Now that I think about it, it's kind of like the magi who spent years traveling just to see Baby Jesus.

Merry Barackmas,
Chris

January 1, 2009

Dear Obama,

Novim Godom! Happy New Year from the Russian Federation. Have you received a call from Medvedev yet? I hope so. I'm starting to envy the governmental structure over there, particularly the "freedom" they have to issue Presidential Decrees. This is similar to our executive order, a privilege you should take advantage of whenever you feel the slightest bit of resistance.

So what are your New Year's resolutions? You might laugh at mine, but I believe it's going to help me tremendously in understanding and following your ideology. I will give you a hint. I started growing out my beard—any guesses? I've been putting on some extra weight—anything? Here's the last hint: I've been going around confronting people about the plight of the worker. If your answer started with the name Karl, you win an all-expense paid trip to your nearest labor camp (ha ha). Speaking of, any updates on the completion date?

Yes, that's right, I'm attempting to morph into Karl Marx. Actually, it's more like character acting. Nevertheless, I plan to take this very seriously. I've done extensive research and have learned various interesting facts about him. One little bit of trivia: he had a ferocious appetite for Knublewurst sausages and pickled sauerkraut, which by the way, I've been consuming at an alarming rate. The result may very well include health problems, but it's a small price to pay for ideological exceptionalism.

It's only been a few days, but I feel I'm on the right track. I'll admit that introducing myself to strangers, as Karl is deceptive and a bit egotistical. Yet it's all part of the process. I only wish I had the luxury of hanging out with like-minded individuals for encouragement like you did during your college years. I believe it was in your first book, *Dreams from My Father*, where you wrote, "I chose my friends carefully. The foreign students. The Chicanos. The Marxist professors and structural feminist, etc." This is one of my favorite passages in your book, both inspiring and telling.

As an example of how serious I am, I recently went out of my comfort zone in search of my fellow brethren. Two days ago I was at Denny's. When my waiter walked up, I was immediately intrigued. He appeared to have this oppressive-chic thing going on. So, I decided to take a chance as I placed my order: "I would like a Marxist Club, hold the Consumerism." After a few seconds of silence I panicked and changed my order to "Moons over my Hammy." I don't know what I expected from him. Maybe I thought he would respond with, "Would you like a side of hope and change with that?" Oh well, I'd probably have better luck at an Abercrombie & Fitch anyway.

One thing is for sure—this isn't going to be a cakewalk. I'm well aware of that. I wish there was a magic pill you could take, but we'll just have to wait until we have nationalized health care for that. For now I have to assume my journey is going to take me on a wild and crazy ride. Who knows what the road will look like?

I feel like I'm close to being a Socialist. I may be an amateur Socialist by definition, but we all know that it is the "Gateway Ideology." I'm hoping to get lucky and head straight to Marxism, but who's to say I won't go straight towards hard-Maoism for a weekend. After that I could easily see myself shooting over to soft-MichaelMooreism for a bender or two. It wouldn't surprise me if I relapsed back to mild-consumerism around the holidays and kids' birthdays, but immediately return to anti-capitalism after the holiday sales. It's conceivable that I might jump headlong into neo-DiCaprioism as cap and trade talks *heat up* (ha ha). However, I could accidentally eat some funny looking mushrooms and end up a modern-Olbermannist.

I just don't know ...

Sincerely hopeful,
Chris

January 5, 2009

Dear Obama,

Sorry to hear Bill Richardson withdrew his Commerce Secretary nomination because of his alleged involvement in a "pay-to-play" scheme. The Federal Grand Jury in New Mexico is investigating if he possibly steered state bond business from the New Mexico Financial Authority to David Rubin, a significant campaign contributor. He pushed state business worth nearly $1.5 million toward CDR Financial products in 2004. Members in your administration mocked his weak attempt at corruption.
 On a brighter note, fantastic pick in Leon Panetta for CIA Director. You really eased the public's fears when you defended this appointee and highlighted his experience saying, "He is smart and has excellent managerial skills." Lucky for us Home Depot didn't scoop him up first.

Sincerely,
Chris

DEAR OBAMA

"Those who cast the votes decide nothing. Those who count the votes decide everything."

– Joseph Stalin

January 10, 2009

Dear Obama,

Al Franken wins! Well, he won the recount. We still have to maneuver through all of the legal loopholes. But barring any honest and legitimate record keeping, he should be the next senator of the great state of Minnesota. The Gopher State should be proud of the results. It's quite clear his message of "Dope and Porn" resonated with the people. Franken, whose successes include a brief stint on *Saturday Night Live* and breathing, will no doubt add to the sanity in Washington these days.

You knew this was going to be a nail-biter from the very beginning. I was a little concerned by the initial results, but feel better now after voting officials/operatives found 100 votes for Franken in the trunk of a car. Thankfully, not one of them was a vote for Norm Coleman. What are the odds on that?

They also continue to find handwritten votes for Franken on random pieces of paper. Minnesota Secretary of State, Mark Ritchie (D) plans to count these votes until Franken is declared the winner, or until DNC volunteers develop writer's cramp. With any luck, Franken will be off to Washington and representing the Hempbelt in no time.

DEAR OBAMA

And let me just say, hats off to Bellevue State Hospital for their flexibility in allowing Franken time to campaign. Their work release program is obviously ahead of its time. I believe it's also in negotiations with Washington to allow Franken time to travel back to Bellevue every other Friday for his beloved Arts & Crafts Day. They're calling it a political furlough program, an outlet that's been missing in Washington for years.

What I find most exciting about this turn of events is the future of the Democratic Party in Minnesota. Franken's success has the DNC on such a high that it's already looking forward to the next election cycle. Early polling has famed Russian funny man Yakov Smirnoff as a major player and contender in 2010, although he is getting a run for his money from the old comic workhorse, Gallagher. Experts are urging caution. They claim all prognostications will be thrown out the window if Carrot Top decides to jump into the race.

Sincerely,
Chris

January 11, 2009

Dear Obama,

Al Franken is a United States Senator.

Sincerely,
Chris

DEAR OBAMA

January 12, 2009

Dear Obama,

I'm impressed. When asked about the escalating violence in Gaza, you made no comment—that was a smart move. Why give people any idea of where you stand on the most important foreign policy situation in the world? I'm hoping it's a prelude to how you're going to handle all foreign policy issues. If I'm reading you right, it appears that you have based your foreign policy on the old adage, "Ignore the problem and it will go away."

If I can make a suggestion (although I'm sure you've already thought of this), I would wait until tensions ease or the conflict resolves itself. Then I would schedule a big news conference. I would hold up a piece of paper and declare, "This was my detailed strategy on how to handle the crisis in the Middle East. My written plan of action is exactly what solved this problem." Then without delay, burn that blank piece of paper.

Another idea is to appoint someone "Update Czar." This person would report daily, weekly, and monthly updates on the Middle East. I was thinking of someone like Tareq Aziz, Saddam Hussein's old media spokesman. I believe we can all recall this colorful figure from the initial invasion of Iraq. I remember appreciating his positivity and passion as he flooded the airwaves with updates on how the Iraqi Army was winning the war and killing tens of thousands of US soldiers. I bring him up as an example of the type of propagandist you could use regarding the Gaza situation. You need to get word out to the rest of the world that everything is fine and peace has ultimately won out in Gaza. Even if it hasn't, I think the power of positive thinking would go a long way.

Definitely something to consider . . .

Sincerely,
Chris

January 17, 2009

Dear Obama,

Three more days—you can feel the excitement growing each and every day. I see the tab for this little soirée is up to about $150 million, not that outrageous for a 45-minute event. You're well past W's total for his 2004 inauguration. I'm sure you remember the backlash when the media discovered the total cost of his party. Who can forget their outrage at all the money spent for such an event, and how they complained that the money could have gone to soldier's protective gear, or thirty to forty brand-new Humvees? I think it's fair to say that with the money spent for your inauguration you could probably buy at least thirty to forty Senate seats, or possibly even 150 state-of-the-art teleprompters.

Let me take a moment and say how proud I am of you and your team for sticking to your promise of complete transparency, or as you so eloquently put it, "Seat at the table of transparency policy." By the way, is that "table" at the Kremlin by any chance? I remember just after the election John Podesta, your transition co-chair, issued this statement about transparency of any meetings, "the date and organizations represented at official meetings in the Transition headquarters or agency offices would be posted on our Web site, at www.change.gov."

We are still anxiously waiting for you to post on your website any and all of your transition meetings with various groups. Your transition spokesman, Nick Shapiro explained why meetings haven't been posted when he said:

> This policy is part of President-elect Obama's commitment to run the most open and transparent transition in history. The transition staff has been instructed that this is a floor and not a ceiling. No transition has ever attempted to implement such disclosure requirements, and as we continue to evaluate the policy, refinements will be made to it.

Oh well, we the people don't need to be bogged down with such minutia...

The only real transparency on the website to speak of so far was this text message exchange between Vice President-elect Joe Biden, and former Secretary of State Madeline Albright. Here is the transcript:

Albright: good luck on tuesday jb
Biden: thanks maddie
Albright: r u nervous?
Biden: not really, more upset
Albright: upset! y?

DEAR OBAMA

Biden: oh nothing, barack and i got into it a little
Albright: about what?
Biden: i wanted to shorten the inauguration ball, u know, for idol
Albright: he didn't go for it?
Biden: nope. "just tivo it joe," he said
Albright: that makes sense
Biden: i don't have the room, u know, gossip girl, etc
Albright: u 2 seem frosty, what gives?
Biden: conflict of ideas
Albright: about your role as vp?
Biden: it's that obvious?
Albright: what have you proposed?
Biden: square dance lessons for the white house staff
Albright: OMG!! i love it
Biden: of course, anybody would, b didn't c the value in it
Albright: exercise 4 one
Biden: exactly, u may want to look into it
Albright: excuse me?
Biden: god love ya!
Albright: what r u talking about?
Biden: have you tried the new orange flavored Metamucil?
Biden: maddie?
Biden: come on maddie
Biden: talk to me
Biden: BFF my ass

Sincerely,
Chris

DEAR OBAMA

"The American people will never knowingly adopt Socialism. But under the name "liberalism" they will adopt every fragment of the socialist program, until one day America will be a Socialist nation, without knowing how it happened."

– Norman Thomas, American Socialist and 6-time US Presidential candidate

January 19, 2009

Dear Obama,

Well this is it, less than 24 hours until you're sworn in. I just want to take this time and say what an honor and privilege it's been to have you as this country's President-elect. As I've documented, no one has come close to what you have achieved while not actually being in office. Of course, one of the highlights of the past couple of months—and what I feel is a glimpse as to what kind of leader you will be—was your all-important and grueling decision to go with the Labradoodle as the White House dog. A landmark decision that I, and many others, felt was underreported.

There have been so many high points since we elected you that I would like to go over a few. I want to focus on your administration picks. I know, I know, I should talk about that jump shot of yours. Believe me, I could write a whole book on how sweet it is. Thankfully the media are doing an adequate job covering it. Here is a summary of your unprecedented appointees who will ultimately drive this country straight into the ground—in a good way, of course . . .

Eric Holder (Attorney General): His claim to fame is the pardon of tax embezzler, Marc Rich. When criticized by both sides of the aisle, Holder explained that he was confused at the time because Mr. Rich has two first names. Holder's other notable achievement is the pardoning of sixteen FALN terrorists. This was another controversial decision since there was actual footage of the men making bombs. After seeing the fuzzy footage of the terrorists "at work," he defended his decision and claimed that they were just building an Erector set. He enjoys rearranging and organizing his extensive Pokémon card collection.

Leon Panetta (CIA Director): With no intelligence background, Mr. Panetta was appointed to head up the Central Intelligence Agency. He's vehemently against all the interrogation methods, which President Bush recklessly used to keep America safe. Waterboarding and Rendition are off-limits. Instead, he plans to gather critical information by serving terrorists curdled milk and overcooked pasta. Already showing toughness and resolve, he is standing behind his plan despite mounting pressure from the ACLU. It has called the proposed practice, "barbaric and intolerable" and has also threatened a lawsuit. Panetta is a huge movie buff and claims to have seen *Tremors 5: The Thunder from Down Under* over 97 times.

Carol Browner ("Climate Czar"): She goes by Mrs.

Browner, or the "EPA freak formerly known as Carol." She comes to us, as one of the former fourteen leaders of the Socialist group, Commission for a Sustainable World Society. This organization calls for "Global Governance" and believes that rich countries must shrink their economies to address climate change. Her appointment does not require a Senate confirmation. She is working on a television pilot for Hollywood titled, "SuperGovernMan." The plot centers on a superhero that fights against freedom and liberty, while meddling in the lives of everyday Americans.

Timothy Geithner (Treasury Secretary): He failed to pay taxes to the IRS and is now in charge of the IRS. While working at the IMF (International Monetary Fund) for four years, he paid neither Social Security nor Medicare taxes (he signed a contract saying he did pay). Keeping in line with Obama's new ethics rules, he wants his top aide at the Treasury Department to be a lobbyist from Goldman Sachs. His youthful looks and intellect almost landed him a role as Hannah Montana's love interest. He enjoys playing Atari, wiffle ball, and of course, tax evading.

Hilda Solis (Secretary of Labor): Longtime supporter of coercive unionism, Solis was tapped to head the Labor Department. In 1996, when she was a California State Senator, she was quoted saying, "We are all Americans whether you are legalized or not." An article in the Communist Party USA's *People's Weekly World* newspaper has since welcomed her as a "great choice" and an "outstanding" selection with a "life-long commitment to working people." She is a strong supporter of increased governmental oversight including taxing and regulating sunshine. She has an intense fear of clogs and was once hospitalized for a severe case of hives after watching Ivy Sands perform Double Hornpipes.

Arne Duncan (Secretary of Education): He's your personal friend and former supporter/recipient of the failed Chicago Annenberg Challenge. In 2001, Mayor Daley appointed him to run Chicago's public schools. According to the US Department of Education's National Assessment of Educational Progress (NAEP) report for 2007, Chicago public schools have consistently performed below the national average, despite having one of the most expensive budgets in the country. In 2008, he supported opening a gay, lesbian, and transgender high school. The project failed and Duncan was immediately encouraged by the board of supervisors to start breaking the Prozac in half. Having recovered from that setback, Arne continues to promote the public schools' current curriculum—ensuring it teaches America's children the important skills of reading, writing, arithmetic and putting a condom on a cucumber.

David Ogden (Deputy Attorney General): If appointed, David would be second in command at the Department of Justice. He has a distinguished law career with the following highlights. He co-authored a brief for the American Psychological Association (APA) arguing that parental notification was an unconstitutional burden on fourteen-year-old girls seeking an abortion. He co-authored

DEAR OBAMA

another brief on behalf of the APA defending "safe sex" education that teaches about oral and anal sex claiming, "Homosexuality is simply one normal variant of sexual identity." He opposed the Child Internet Protection Act (CIPA) stating, "Imposition of mandatory filtering on public libraries impairs the ability of librarians to fulfill the purpose of public libraries—namely, assisting library patrons in their quest for information … " His clients include the porn industry, ACLU, and pro-abortion groups. Before accepting the Deputy Attorney General position, he was a partner at the law firm Schmuckman, Degeneratsky & Gutterstein.

Steven Chu (Secretary of Energy): Steven's a Nobel Prize winner and a big global warming advocate. He nearly won a second Nobel Prize for his advanced theory, "Global Warming: It Sucks!" He shocked the scientific community when he concluded that global warming increases inexplicably every year between the months of June and August. He became so engrossed in his work that he began referring to global warming as "Margaret," and was often heard shouting from a nearby hillside, "You never loved me!" He is a member of the Al Gore Fan Club, and loves to participate in the clubs various activities including: hysteria workshops, buffet crashing, monotone training, and the consumption of pale tablets.

Proud American,
Chris

DEAR OBAMA

"There were over 1 million people at the inauguration and only 18 missed work."

– Unknown

January 21, 2009

Dear Obama,

I couldn't sleep a wink last night. I've never witnessed something so moving in my entire life. There are simply no words to describe yesterday's inauguration. I didn't know what to expect, but somehow I expected it. Sound corny? Nevertheless, it was a day that this country will remember forever, and I mean forever.

I sat there in awe as the cameras scanned the entire Lincoln Memorial. It was an amazing scene as people from all walks of life converged to celebrate this historic event. I was inspired as I saw the sea of sixties hippies mingling with modern day Bolsheviks and substance-riddled youths rubbing shoulders with guilt-ridden elites. People battled freezing temperatures just to be a part of history.

Watching the coverage you would have thought you had grown up in circumstances similar to the slums of Mumbai. Sadly your mother was a well-traveled anthropologist with a Ph.D. from the University of Hawaii, and your father only had a degree from the University of Hawaii and an MBA from Harvard.

Living with your grandparents in Hawaii must have been difficult. I'm sure food stamps were commonplace, as the only source of income was the meager wages your grandmother earned as vice president of the Bank of Hawaii. Clearly since you had to attend the exclusive Punahou High School in Honolulu you became just another statistic floundering in the private educational system. I applaud the media for bringing to light your humble beginnings and giving hope to all those children who have wealthy, highly-educated parents and family members.

It all makes for one heck of a story Mr. President, and that's why I commend MSNBC's, Chris Matthews who displayed one of the more touching moments last night. While you were being sworn in, he quietly stood up, pointed to you on the big screen and whispered, "You complete me." I'm sure Matthews was not the only one expressing such emotion, and I would have certainly witnessed more had my wife not changed the channel to *Saved by the Bell.*

Best of luck Mr. President (and America)...

Sincerely,
Chris

P.S. When you proposed to Michelle, did you use a teleprompter?

DEAR OBAMA

"One does not establish a dictatorship in order to safeguard a revolution; one makes a revolution in order to establish a dictatorship."

– George Orwell

January 22, 2009

Dear Obama,

Some people are saying that you're already acting like a dictator. Of course, this isn't even close to being true. As far as I can tell, you are ruling as an absolute monarch who is not challenged or restrained by any agency and whose ultimate goal is to create a single party state that forbids criticism or opposition to the government. We're talking a Gala to a Granny Smith here ...

I suppose some might point to the five executive orders you've given within the first three days as President (I see you have taken my suggestion). One might call you an "Executive Order Pez Dispenser" because of the speed in which you've handed them down—the previous six presidents had only two combined. I disagree with this characterization and say that at worst, you barely resemble a "mini" dictator. Before anyone jumps to any conclusions, let's wait and see how many more you authorize. We still haven't finished out the week.

There are so many other stories going around right now that I hate to focus on such an insignificant one. Nobody is even talking about your first official phone call which was to Mahmoud Abbas, the leader of the terrorist party, Fatah.

I believe you said, "This is my first phone call to a foreign leader." Not bad.

I think you sent a strong message when you signed the executive order delaying the planned execution of 9/11 mastermind, Khalid-Sheik Mohammad. If he's smart, he will now take his case to civilian court where he has a good chance of getting off on a technicality. With any luck, he will soon be granted asylum and will end up working at a delicatessen on the upper Eastside.

Your swift action to draw up plans to close Gitmo sent another powerful warning to our enemies. You intend to give the sworn enemies of this country the same constitutional rights as American citizens. How will they ever endure the rigors of our civilian courts, acquittal, and living among the general public? I hope that if they are not able to find gainful employment after they are released that they will have the opportunity to seek one of Nancy Pelosi's SCHIP programs and apply for welfare. After all, it wouldn't be fair if they couldn't find a job.

This all leads me to tell you about an idea I've been mulling. I've been thinking that it might be beneficial to use federal money to create an Adopt-a-Terrorist Program. Since you're closing Gitmo and most likely some of those secret prisons, you will need to find adequate housing for these folks. I believe there are plenty of good progressive couples out there who are interested in becoming part of the solution. For those not able to actually adopt, you could have some sort of mentor program, like a Big Brother/Sister sort of thing where a nice couple from Cambridge could show a terrorist what it's like to be a citizen of this great country. They could take them to

DEAR OBAMA

Fenway Park, on a famous Duck Tour of Boston, or perhaps even have them participate in a Rainbow Coalition parade. Such experiences might help change their minds and cause them to think twice about hating America.

Maybe sharing a cup of coffee and a raised glazed at Dunkin' Donuts could assuage 1,000 years of animosity?

Sincerely,
Chris

January 24, 2009

Dear Obama,

For some odd reason I've been down in the dumps lately. I guess I'm just feeling a little nostalgic. You've done so much for the country, and it's all going to be over in eight years. I know I should take each day at a time, but some days just seem to be harder than others. My only solace is that you will consider revising or eliminating the 22nd Amendment (Presidential term limits).

I have a feeling George Soros, Rahm Emanuel, or even John Podesta might have something in the works. At least I'm hoping they do. If I had to bet, I think Soros has something up his sleeve. I just don't know what. Whatever it is, I'm sure he has America's best interest at heart.

I'm not kidding about that 22nd Amendment. Have your advisors get creative. Trust me, it can be done. Besides, no one really cares about those amendments in the twenties anyway. All the good ones are in the top thirteen or fourteen. Now I know the mere suggestion of this makes you cringe, and I have no doubt you would fight this with every fiber of your being, but just imagine years and years of unfettered governmental intrusion.

Promise me you will at least think about it . . .

Sincerely,
Chris

January 28, 2009

Dear Obama,

In case you were wondering I stopped my character acting of Karl Marx. It's just too much right now. I had no idea how much of an intellectual he was. The different theories he had on destroying wealth and capitalism and keeping one's dream down were just too complex—plus my cholesterol hit 270.

Grieving failure,
Chris

DEAR OBAMA

"How do you tell a communist? It's someone who reads Marx and Lenin, and how do you tell an anti-communist? It's someone who understands Marx and Lenin."

– Ronald Reagan

February 1, 2009

Dear Obama,

As disappointed as I am in my failed Karl Marx experiment, it hasn't deterred me from my ultimate goal of becoming a balding revolutionary. Your inspirational victory alone is a great reminder to never get down, to never lose sight of your dreams, and to discard reason when convenient.

The KM setback is certainly discouraging, but I'm forging on. I went back to the basics and purchased some supportive reading material. The first two pieces of literature I picked up are near and dear to your heart. You know I'm talking about *Das Kapital* and *Rules for Radicals*. I also purchased two other books, but decided to return *American History* and *The Fundamentals of the U.S. Constitution*.

I started with *Das Kapital,* and one of the first exciting tidbits I learned about was "Psychological Repression." This is the psychological act of excluding desires and impulses from one's consciousness (i.e. Joe Biden's impulse to lick a frozen signpost).

"Political Repression" was another main theme and

common among your everyday dictator. Examples of this would include forced disappearances and other extrajudicial punishments for political activists, dissidents, or oppositions in the general population. You might want to pass this idea along to Rahm Emanuel.

There are plenty of other applicable passages in the book. One that intrigues me, as I'm sure it intrigues you, is this: "All products contain value that is directly proportional to the amount of labor embodied within them." Isn't there a quote that calls money the "common whore of mankind?" I'm starting to see the truth behind this, especially since I don't have any money.

As influential as *Das Kapital* is, I know most of your ideology and "strategery" (ha ha) is from the Great Saul Alinsky. I've barely started *Rules for Radicals* and already I feel like I'm reading your senior thesis or current playbook. The practical information could easily be applied to my bald campaign. I haven't had much time to get it off the ground, but now that I have this as a resource …

I know it is a fact that you are an Alinskyite and spent years teaching workshops on his methods. It was thoughtful and must have meant a lot to you to have Saul's own son, David send you that letter saying, "Obama learned his lesson well. I'm proud to see that my father's model for organizing is being applied successfully beyond local community organizing to affect the Democratic campaign in 2008. It is a fine tribute to Saul Alinsky as we approach his 100th birthday." Wow—how beautiful and inspirational.

I have to admit that I was a little confused as to how you were going to govern the country, but again this book puts it all into perspective. With nationalized health care, cap and trade, government ownership of financial institutions, census control, etc., this all falls in line with one of the main points of *Rules for Radicals*, "Create mass organizations to seize power; to realize the democratic dream of equality, justice, peace …"

Your anti-corporation campaign, highlighted by the recent uproar of the AIG bonuses and subsequent government intervention in seizing its funds, is explained in the section on tactics. Alinsky states, "Here our concern is with the tactic of taking; how the Have-Nots can take power from the Haves."

If I may, let me close out by quoting the dedication from your political bible, *Rules for Radicals*:

> Lest we forget at least an over-the-shoulder acknowledgement to the very first radical: from all our legends, mythology, and history … the first radical known to man who rebelled against the establishment and did it so effectively that he at least won his own kingdom – Lucifer.

This is one American who will be sleeping well tonight . . .

Sincerely,
Chris

DEAR OBAMA

February 3, 2009

Dear Obama,

Sorry to hear about Tom Daschle. What a circus, eh? It was plastered all over the QVC and TeleMundo channels. I'm just glad to hear that he is "sorry" for not paying $140,000 in taxes. I'll have to remember the "sorry defense" in case I ever get into tax trouble.

I don't know why he withdrew his nomination over this. Treasury Secretary Geithner had the same "hiccup" and breezed through the confirmations. Oh well, it would have been nice to have yet another lobbyist in your administration (Daschle, of course, being a lobbyist for the health care industry). Actually, you could have had a husband and wife team. Daschle's wife was a very successful lobbyist as well.

At least you added some stability to the day by scheduling a news conference to announce a new middle class task force. Naturally, you tapped our very own Vice President, Joe Biden. Who better to lead this task force than someone who has never had a real job?

Sincerely,
Chris

DEAR OBAMA

February 5, 2009

Dear Obama,

Trumped up tax problems continue to plague your appointees. Today's public servant is your pick for Labor Secretary, Hilda Solis. I previously documented her qualifications in my entry highlighting a few of your administration all-stars. Had I been aware the well-known socialist member had tax issues I would have added it to her already impressive resume.

The Right is already hammering you over this. I wish they could be honest with themselves for one second and realize that had there been any Democrats left that have actually paid their taxes you would have considered them.

I'm wondering if there is any way Charlie Rangel, Chairman of the House Ways and Means Committee and currently under investigation for not paying his own taxes, could quit his leadership position. You could then immediately appoint him back to his chairmanship and continue this streak of appointing patriotic tax-dodgers. Ironically, Rep. Rangel is currently in charge of writing the country's new tax laws.

I have to admit things do appear to be unraveling. Your pledge to bring this divisive nation together has been slightly derailed. It's clear you have allowed this to happen. Despite the issues with your appointees and all the gridlock on Capitol Hill, you know what the future holds. With that being said, I have an idea that I believe might help in creating that image of unity you've been seeking.

I was thinking you could have someone design team

jerseys for your new administration to wear—you know—something that can hammer home this talk of unity. I'm envisioning orange jumpsuits with a little identification number stenciled on their backs. You could even appoint a team leader to help facilitate this sense of togetherness. Rod Blagojevich is someone who immediately comes to mind. Who better to hand out welcome packets, lead tours, and answer any questions about morning role call? I suspect the American people would not object to such a proposal.

Sincerely,
Chris

February 10, 2009

Dear Obama,

I was having a bad morning until I heard about your victory on the Stimulus Bill. The news couldn't have come at a better time for me. Not that anything major happened, but this little funk almost kept me from writing today. I guess it's just one of those days when the world seemed so orderly and in control.

The thing that got me started was that while on my way to work this morning, a truck passed me with a bumper sticker that read, "Frodo failed, Obama has the Ring." Even worse, he was driving one of those behemoth trucks that on its own could probably melt a glacier.

As a *Lord of the Rings* enthusiast, this was offensive on many different levels. The most glaring is that we all know

DEAR OBAMA

Frodo did not fail in his mission to destroy the ring at Narnia. And frankly, had the roles been reversed you would have succeeded in half the time it took Frodo and Voldemort ... or something.

Again, thank you for coming through at crunch time on your Stimulus Bill. I, along with dozens of others, salute you. I knew all of your whining and complaining would result in a win. I must admit, it's a little awkward to see you go from a man of strength and hope to a leader of doom and gloom. But hey, you had to pull out all the guns to get this one through. If it meant acting like a four year-old and blaming everything on Congress and saying, "I inherited this and that," then so be it. I just can't wait to tell my five year-old that he gets to be "patriotic" and pay for all this when he is older. He'll be as excited as I am.

By the way, if I were you, I would immediately suspend all aid, resources, goodwill, and other benefits to the Czech Republic. I was outraged when EU President and Czech Prime Minister, Mirek Topolánek told the European Parliament that President Obama's monstrous stimulus package and backing bailouts "is the road to hell." Number one, this is a completely outrageous and unacceptable remark. Number two, it's factually incorrect—we all know the road to hell is the I-15 on the way to Vegas.

Fun Fact: Despite several nominations, Legolas (*Lord of the Rings* fame) has never won an Emmy for his role as Bill Maher on HBO's *Real Time with Bill Maher*.

Sincerely,
Chris

DEAR OBAMA

"I have always loved longitude. I love latitude; it's in the stars. But longitude, it's about time ... Time and clocks and all the rest of that have always been a fascination for me."

– Speaker of the House, Nancy Pelosi

February 12, 2009

Dear Obama,

I don't know about you, but since you've inherited such a miserable situation I think it's only fair that we extend your honeymoon period from the first 100 days to the first 4 years.

Speaking of fair, how about our illustrious Speaker of the House, Nancy Pelosi? Is she all about compromise and doing what's best for the American people or what? I love how she handles herself. Our California girl is smart, personable, and surprisingly casual, as she is often seen addressing Congress in her Ugg Boots. It's hard for an outsider to understand just how much her intellect and discourse is valued in D.C. She certainly is one of a kind, and will no doubt be missed as she transitions from the political arena to being a full time blogger.

Her blog, "StretchForSuccess," should be up and running sometime in 2012. Most assume she will continue to add to the political discourse through this medium. They also expect Speaker Pelosi will focus more on her areas of expertise (women's rights and business) which were both highlighted by her recent statement, "Birth control will help the economy."

There are some who are concerned that Speaker Pelosi is suffering from an early onset of Collette Reardon Syndrome. Collette Reardon was the prescription drug junkie character played by former *Saturday Night Live* actress, Cheri Oteri. So far she has exhibited the most basic and obvious signs: the clueless smile, the frantic eyes, and the erratic speech. Some fear it's only a matter of time before she is seen careening down the hallways of the Capitol building with a shopping cart covered in lipstick.

The only way to confirm this would be to do a complete blood work panel on Speaker Pelosi. Until this happens, medical experts will have to continue their own unsolicited diagnoses. Based on her speech and demeanor, the doctors believe that a sample of Mrs. Pelosi's blood might resemble the Periodic Table, and/or Pfizer's 2010 Product Catalog. In an act of cowardice, some of her so-called colleagues have drafted a silent referendum, that if approved would legally change her position from "Speaker of the House" to "Tweaker of the House." Such a suggestion is both outrageous and probably accurate.

Ironically, New York Senator, Chuck Schumer has taken on the name Mr. Peepers. Now this is not to be confused with Chris Kattan's character from SNL, although he does share many of his attributes. In Mr. Schumer's case, it was the name given to him by his neighbors and some of the women down at the community pool.

Sincerely,
Chris

DEAR OBAMA

February 16, 2009

Dear Obama,

Tell Vice President Biden I was sorry to hear that no one participated in the Flash mob he organized on the Senate floor today. I still commend him for finishing the song.

Bored,
Chris

February 22, 2009

Dear Obama,

I have a sneaking suspicion that White House Press Secretary, Robert Gibbs is a Mensa member. I have no hard evidence to support my claim, other than hours of raw media footage depicting a man with an uncanny grasp of the English language. His exceptional clarity and fluidity in expressing his thoughts has this highly intellectual organization written all over him. I don't expect him to admit it anytime soon considering all the humility coming out of your administration these days.

Sincerely,
Chris

DEAR OBAMA

"The truth is that men are tired of liberty."

– Benito Mussolini

February 28, 2009

Dear Obama,

I know you won't be able to get this message from me, but your website was down earlier—the website that is supposed to have all the transparency you've promised. There is still nothing posted except for another random text message. Unfortunately, it was cut off about half way through.

Albright:	good luck with the middle class job
Biden:	the what?
Albright:	the new task force u r leading
Biden:	nice try maddie, u ever used the sham-wow?
Albright:	no
Biden:	this thing works like crap
Albright:	use a paper towel
Biden:	try scam-wow
Albright:	how's the prez?
Biden:	he's mad again
Albright:	what is it this time?
Biden:	oh, i taped over some sensitive national security material
Albright:	with what?
Biden:	paul blart mall cop

DEAR OBAMA

Albright: OMG
Biden: whatever, u r looking gr8 by the way
Albright: just a diet warrior these days
Biden: r u doing that clay aiken diet?
Albright: u mean atkins diet?
Biden: the what?

Sincerely,
Chris

February 29, 2009

Dear Obama,

For years I've been reluctant to blame my baldness on George W. Bush. I had always accepted the notion that it was genetic and passed on through your mother's father. It is true that my grandfather was bald, but I think that's only half the story. I recently looked at some old photos from the past eight years. What was astounding is that my hair loss accelerated at a far greater pace during his tenure than at any other time ... damn him.

What do you think of the idea for a soap opera called, *The Bald and the Beautiful*?

Oh, what's the point—no one's listening ...

Frustrated,
Chris

DEAR OBAMA

March 1, 2009

Dear Obama,

What do you think the reaction from pro-choice supporters would be if we discovered a fossilized amoeba on Mars? Celebration and euphoria would be my guess, based on how infatuated people are with "extraterrestrial" life. What if instead they found an aborted fetus on Mars? Once again, I would still say celebration and euphoria. How could it not be? To discover other life forms as progressive as we are ... please.

You finally brought Kansas Governor, Kathleen Sebelius on board. She was always my top choice for the Health and Human Services post. I kept asking myself, "When is the President going to bring Sebelius into his administration?" She is qualified to serve in just about any capacity for this country. In fact, some even thought she was going to be your pick for Vice President.

Sadly, she might get a little push back during the confirmation hearings because of her so-called extremist views on abortion. I see nothing different between her stance on abortion and yours. You both believe in the Born Alive Act, which orders medical staff to deny a failed aborted baby care until it dies—something any civilized country should endorse.

I'm certain the biggest controversy will center on her relationship with late-term abortionist, George Tiller. In 2007 she hosted a party exclusively for Tiller and his staff at the Governor's mansion, even though he was under investigation at the time for his illegal practices. As

DEAR OBAMA

Governor of the State of Kansas, I'm sure she had no idea what was going on. I'm also sure, if you ask anyone, they would say, "big deal," let the Governor enjoy a nice evening of dinner and drinks with the Manson family.

Assuming she breezes through confirmation, her first order of business will most likely be to extend the Born Alive Act to six to twelve months post birth (The Botched Child Rearing Decision). It seems perfectly acceptable that if you give birth to a baby, and after six months you're not happy with it, then you should have the right to abort it. How is one to know if they're going to like child rearing if they've never experienced it before? What if new parents are considerably more tired than they anticipated or they're not making happy hour as frequently as they used to? These are questions that need to be addressed.

Once and for all, let's put the controversy to rest: Life officially begins at the point of carbon neutrality . . .

Sincerely,
Chris

March 4, 2009

Dear Obama,

I thought you might get a kick that we have an over/under pool running at work right now on how many executive orders you will sign during the first 100 days of your presidency. We set it at 35. And let me just reiterate that you are not a dictator. A dictator would have signed at least one or two more orders than you have by now. Besides, the order you're going to sign on Monday shouldn't even be considered an executive order. Embryonic stem cell research should never have been restricted in the first place.

If we have to be honest, it never really was restricted. It's difficult to remember that based on media coverage. They would lead us to believe that President Bush made it illegal to do research on Embryonic Stem Cells, when what he did was not allow federal funds for research. He believed that the federal government shouldn't be in the practice of making moral judgments, which is a crock.

I find it hard to imagine that Americans would object to you making moral decisions for the entire country. The American people just have to stop listening to their conscience and realize that destroying life with their tax dollars is actually a good thing. Even though all of the scientific breakthroughs have come from adult stem cells and umbilical cord stem cells, we need to throw as much federal money as possible at embryonic research until we get results, or even if we don't.

At least it makes everyone feel good if we try. . .

Sincerely,
Chris

DEAR OBAMA

March 6, 2009

Dear Obama,

What a busy Friday! Normally things quiet down towards the end of the week, but not this week. In one day we had the unemployment report, Sanjay Gupta withdrawing from the Surgeon General post, more heat on NIC appointee Chas Freeman, and a report that says you're definitely going to sign another executive order overturning the ban on embryonic stem cell research.

We all know the unemployment report takes center stage. The 8.1% is not going to give the markets or the country much confidence. I'll tell you what will though— inviting the co-founder of Twitter to participate in a business conference at the White House. It's obviously crunch time now and you've decided to bring in the big guns. Upon hearing that he was invited, Ev Williams said (through a tweet of course), "[this] must mean they're *really* out of ideas." I can't seem to put my finger around why people are losing confidence in your ability to help the economy.

I noticed that the Right is making up another bogus controversy. This time it's regarding your pick for Chairman of the National Intelligence Board (NIC), Charles (Chas) Freeman. Here we have a man who after a distinguished diplomatic career, decides to jump in bed with the Saudis and give into all their demands in exchange for lucrative support for his research center and consulting firm.

Call me old fashioned, but it just sounds like a guy

trying to make an honest buck. And for goodness sake, stop with the anti-Semitism. Just because the MEPC runs the magazine, *Middle East Policy*—that Mr. Freeman basically manages—which has printed several anti-Semitic editorials, it doesn't necessarily mean he has contempt for the Jewish people. And lastly, as an American who bleeds red, white, and blue, I am not the least bit offended that Mr. Freeman is on the board of a major Chinese oil company that is currently in the middle of a multi-billion-dollar Iranian oil deal. Who isn't?

Sincerely,
Chris

P.S. Rumor has it that former DNC chairman and current "Stability Czar," Howard Dean may take the Surgeon General position. I can't think of better way to end a day …

March 7, 2009

Dear Obama,

Another historic day—it was your first meeting with Prime Minister Gordon Brown. Let me just say, "unbelievable." It sounds like everything went very well, especially the gift exchange. Personally, I thought it was a little tacky on Mr. Brown's part to give you a penholder fashioned from the timber of the HMS Gannet, a Navy vessel that served on anti-slavery missions off the coast of Africa. Did he think it was a white elephant exchange? How about that framed commissioning paper for the HMS Resolute, a royal Navy ship that came to symbolize the British-American goodwill when it was rescued by the US from icebergs and given to Queen Victoria? He topped off this embarrassing gift exchange by giving a first edition of Martin Gilbert's seven-volume biography of warmonger Winston Churchill, whose World War II partnership with FDR exemplified the US-Anglo alliance.

All I know is that he must have felt three-feet tall when you gave him your incredibly thoughtful gift. I wish I could have been there to see his reaction when you handed him a Target bag filled with twenty-five DVDs. Aside from the facts that he is not known to be much of a movie buff, or that American DVDs will not work in England, it was a perfect gift to encapsulate the current state of America.

Nothing summarizes our past historic relationships with Thatcher, Churchill, and Blair more than *My Cousin Vinny*. Unfortunately for Mr. Brown, hindsight is 20/20. He didn't realize that historic, meaningful gifts are so cliché these days. I heard that when Prime Minister Brown was thumbing through the DVDs, you elbowed him when he came to *Return of the Jedi* and said, "That's the one with Princess Leia in the gold bikini."

I can only imagine the rigorous vetting that occurred when selecting the movies. Common sense would know that the original *Police Academy* is a given. Obviously it is a classic, but each of the eighteen sequels has its share of hilarious and memorable pranks. Thankfully, that's why you're in the position you're in, to make those tough decisions.

DEAR OBAMA

I would have chosen movies based upon our American politicians, just to give Prime Minister Brown and his wife a little insight into who is governing the United States. For instance, for Vice President Biden I would have chosen *Weekend at Bernie's*. For Hillary Clinton I would have chosen *The Sisterhood of the Travelling Pantsuits*. Timothy Geithner's would have been *Big*. For David Axelrod I would have gone with *Boogie Nights*. Speaker Pelosi's would have been a little more difficult, either *Clueless* or *Misery*. I would leave the ultimate decision up to the vetting team. I'm sure you get the gist. The only question left unanswered is if you remembered to give the Browns the Blockbuster Family Special—popcorn, Red Vines, and Goobers.

Just kidding—I know you would never be that clueless . . .

Closest ally: England
England's gift: rare historical artifacts
America's response: *Caddyshack*
Priceless ...

Sincerely,
Chris

March 12, 2009

Dear Obama,

Madoff pleads guilty to eleven felony charges! He faces a

possible 150 years in prison; I only wish he were a lot younger. The other big news of the day is about your promotion of self-avowed communist, Van Jones to "Green Czar." Technically speaking, he's a special advisor for green jobs, enterprise, and innovation at the White House Council on Environmental Quality. In other words, "Green Czar" is a make believe position that will add more bureaucracy to our already bloated government ... j/k!

I have no doubt that Van is the man for the job. He is a Yale graduate and founder and director of the Bay Area Police Watch. This is a watchdog group that basically keeps the police in check by making sure thugs, criminals, and drug addicts resisting arrest are not subject to harsh language or intense stares. It's been a very successful enterprise and has only cost the city and state a fortune in lawsuits. Once again sir, it's another slam-dunk for your growing list of unelected, unaccountable "Czars."

Those in the know are projecting you will announce a new "Tony Soprano Czar" any day now. This person is to oversee the "Civilian National Security Force." If I had to guess, I suspect you're looking for someone like a Che Guevara or Heinrich Himmler. Personally, I would lean towards someone like Che. He had that flare and panache that Himmler seemed to lack. Himmler just seemed a little too stuffy to me.

Anyway, keep 'em coming . . .

Sincerely,
Chris

DEAR OBAMA

March 14, 2009

Dear Obama,

I was watching *One Flew over the Cuckoo's Nest* last night, and it dawned on me how fortunate we are to have Joe Biden serving as Vice President. During the campaign I wondered how difficult it must be to choose a VP. Stories like the one Richard Ben Cramer shared must have made this decision easier than we all thought: "Joe often didn't know what he thought until he had to say it. In one recent committee debate, recalls an observer, Biden delivered a rambling explanation of his opposition to a foreign aid amendment, by the end of which he had seemed to talk himself out of his original position."

    I recently browsed through Biden's resume and saw how it truly was a no-brainer. He has everything you could want in a Vice President. I compiled a checklist of his qualifications for the archives:

Authenticity (check): In September of 1987 during his presidential run, Biden plagiarized a speech by then leader of the British Labour party, Neil Kinnock. He's also accused of using parts of speeches from President Hoover and Robert Kennedy.

Honesty (check): He bragged during his presidential run in 1988 that he had graduated in the top half of his class at Syracuse Law, when in fact he finished 76th out of 85. He also claimed that he had attended law school on a full scholarship, and had received three degrees in college. He actually earned a single B.A. in History and Political Science and received a half scholarship to law school based on financial needs with some additional assistance based in part upon academics. He also released his undergraduate grades at this time, which were unexceptional. Biden went on *The Early Show* the morning after Louisiana Governor Bobby Jindal gave his response to President Obama's State of the Union address. He said, "What did [Jindal] do? Louisiana is losing 400 jobs a day." When in fact the Louisiana Workforce Commission was quoted in December as saying, "Louisiana was the only state in the nation besides the District of Columbia that added employment over the month."

Health (check): Although he did suffer two brain aneurysms in the late '80s, Mr. Biden is healthy as an ox. One of his aneurysms was so severe that if he hadn't gotten help it would have cost him his life. To this day he still suffers from headaches. By comparison, he is doing much better than sickly John McCain who was given a clean bill of health by numerous doctors and released over a thousand pages of his medical records, which declared him very healthy.

Humility (check): During his presidential run, Biden was asked by a New Hampshire resident about his grades in law school. Biden replied, "I think I probably have a much higher IQ than you do, I suspect."

Smarter than a 5th Grader (check): During a campaign interview with Katie Couric, he commented on how FDR was the president during the Great Depression, even though it was Hoover. He also discussed how FDR addressed the American people on television, during the Depression, despite the fact that TVs weren't invented until the '40s. While campaigning in Missouri, Biden told State Senator Chuck Graham, "Stand up Chuck, let 'em see you." It was a perfectly reasonable request, but unfortunately the Congressman is confined to a wheelchair.

Foreign Policy Experience (check): This is obviously Mr. Biden's bread and butter. He stood against the policies in the '80s to contain the Marxist Sandinistas in Nicaragua. He opposed giving aid to the South Vietnamese government in its war against the North, which led to the fall of an American ally and inevitably the killing fields and genocide of Cambodia. He also went against President Reagan in his effort to confront the former Soviet Union. He voted against the first Gulf War. He also voted against the surge in Iraq, calling it a "tragic mistake." His solution for Iraq was to split the country into three regions: Kurds, Shiites, and Sunnis. The only foreign policy issue in the past thirty years he said he got wrong was the recent war in Iraq, from which our troops will be coming home victorious.

Who says he's not qualified? . . .

Sincerely,
Chris

DEAR OBAMA

March 17, 2009

Dear Obama,

We're 55 days into your administration and you only have 3 of the 25 members of your economic staff filled. Despite being short staffed, your agenda is still getting out there. Christina Romer, former Berkeley professor and current Janet Reno imposter, was on *Meet the Press* this past weekend getting the word out. She was affirming your politically calculated reassessment of the state of the economy. She said the fundamentals of the US economy are strong and that the ingenuity of the American people will be the thing to bring us out of this recession. Basically, that's the same thing John McCain said and was rightfully hammered for it during the presidential campaign.

How could we, the electorate, trust anything that man said? At that time, all we knew about Senator McCain was that he had a checkered past involving radical associations, shady land deals, questionable campaign contributions, a failed community organizing record, a total of two years in the Senate (most of which was spent campaigning), supported infanticide, and had a plethora of fanatical mentors and pastors. I think the American people made it clear that you have to earn their trust. And most importantly, character and integrity will trump a smooth-talking charlatan any day.

Conversely, Mr. President, your record compared to that of the so-called "Maverick" is one of pure love for this great country, highlighted by a lifetime of public service. You spent 22 years serving this country in the Navy, you earned two Medal of Honors, you refused to be released from the Hanoi Hilton unless all of your men accompanied you, you have a strong record of bipartisanship in Washington, you're never afraid to go against your own political party, and you have a wife devoted to philanthropy around the world. It's no surprise the people placed their trust in you. I can only imagine how many out there feel foolish for not giving more credence to the endorsements of Muammar Gaddafi, the Mullahs in Iran, and Busta Rhymes.

It's bad enough that Senator McCain was so close to the presidency, but can you imagine Sarah Palin as Vice President? We barely dodged a disaster with that one. Recently, I read that Alaska's financial institutions are holding up great despite the worsening economy and the recent national bailouts of troubled banks. The "moose killer" probably thinks this is due to her leadership. This woman is so out of touch with reality it's mind-boggling. She acts as if she is the most popular governor in the nation just because she has the highest approval ratings, and a sound state economy.

I hope she has her sights on 2012. Maybe then the media will do their job and dig up the real dirt on this woman and her family. I think we can all agree that there is some unfinished business up there in that backwards state of hers. I trust the *Daily Kos*, *The Huffington Post*, and the *West Beverly Blaze* will do the proper vetting and finally get to the truth about her children.

Sincerely,
Chris

DEAR OBAMA

March 19, 2009

Dear Obama,

Nothing pleases me more than when our leaders act in the best interest of the people. That's why when I saw the headline, "ACORN to Partner with Government for 2010 Census" it brought a chill down my spine ... a comforting chill.

Despite ACORN having a history of voter fraud and embezzlement, it has recently signed on as a national partner with the US Census Bureau, a nonpartisan, non-political agency. Washington State filed felony charges against several paid employees and supervisors for more than 1,700 fraudulent voter registrations. Clearly it was a false accusation, and it was all cleared up after an ACORN spokesman said it wasn't true.

Once it's official, its duties will include recruiting 1.4 million workers who go door to door to count every person in the United States. Mathematical accuracy will be of the utmost importance, as will the absence of political motives. I have no reason to doubt that all recently deceased folks will be properly represented in the census, as well as hardworking illegal aliens.

Skeptics should feel assured that you, Mr. President, have done the only nonpartisan thing you could do and moved the census into the White House (which has never been done before). And let me be clear, I totally disagreed with Republican Congressman Bob Bishop when he said, "He takes something that is supposedly apolitical like the census, and gives it to a guy who is infamously political."

DEAR OBAMA

Of course the Congressman is referring to your Chief of Staff, Rahm Emanuel. Those who've had dealings with Mr. Emanuel in the past know full well that he has nothing but respect for his opposition, even though his nickname is Rahmbo and some describe him as a typical mobster, knee-capper, or Jeff Gillooly wannabe.

I found it humorous that when on the night Clinton was elected in 1992, Mr. Emanuel sat at the dinner table and began ranting at a list of Clinton enemies. As he shouted each name he stabbed the table with his steak knife: "Nat Landow! Dead! ... Cliff Jackson! Dead!" Mr. Bi-Partisan even sent a dead fish to a pollster who made him angry. Sure the previous story could have been right out of an episode of the *Sopranos*, but it's all in good fun. I have all the faith in the world that Rahm Corleone will oversee the census with honor and integrity.

Nevertheless, ACORN has a history of great achievements and deserves this opportunity to serve the public. Some have forgotten that it was one of the main forces behind the Community Reinvestment Act (CRA) that coerced mortgage lenders to make risky loans to minorities and low-income individuals. To this day they brag about the success they had in bringing so many deserving people into mortgages they couldn't afford.

Sincerely,
Chris

P.S. From now on I will refer to Rahm Emanuel as Gillooly— for obvious reasons.

DEAR OBAMA

March 26, 2009

Dear Obama,

Being that you are a master of time, space, and dimension, I'm hesitant to direct any criticism towards you or your administration. Who am I to question someone with such credentials? Nevertheless, I must confront the situation.

It involves the head of your Department of Homeland Security, Janet Napolitano. To be blunt Mr. President, she scares me. She frightens me to my very core. Despite having impeccable credentials to run such a department, this avid hiker and former attorney is setting a precedent that I'm afraid could lead to further alienation from the rest of the world. I feel like she is straight out of the former Soviet Union, or worse, a horrible holdover from W's administration.

The final straw came after she decided to change the phrases "War on Terror" to "Overseas Contingency Operation" and "Terrorist Attack" to "Man-Caused Disaster." I know I'm not alone when I say her actions seem eerily reminiscent of the Iron Curtain. At least I will give her credit for dropping a couple of other phrases that if adopted would have sparked global unrest. Apparently she was considering renaming a terrorist attack, "A Pyrotechnic Extravaganza." She was also very close to renaming a terrorist or enemy combatant as, "A misunderstood individual, with a big heart, who hasn't had proper diversity training." Again, I humbly disagree with this course of action. It totally goes against your campaign message of regaining respect around the world, and getting people to think we're cool again.

Although I'm a little discouraged, I was however pleasantly surprised to see that the House passed a bill allocating billions for your precious "Civilian Security Force." Who knows, you may get that force, modeled after the Pioneer Youth, after all. Let's not get ahead of ourselves. It still has a long way to go before it ever sees the light of day. Even though my sons are young I think they're excited about the prospect of mandatory volunteerism.

Sincerely,
Chris

April 1, 2009

Dear Obama,

What in the world are you doing out there!? An iPod gift for the Queen of England!? If President Bush had given such a gift, the media in this country would have died a thousand deaths. At least you checked your ego at the door and only downloaded 40 of your speeches for her.

Your first few months as President have been a complete and utter disaster. Between the village of tax cheats and radical "Czars" in your administration, the piling up of more debt than all the past presidents combined, the false promises you made regarding no earmarks or lobbyists, strict stem cell guidelines, and transparency, you've managed to make former President

Jimmy Carter look, well, presidential. It's sad when an iPod gift to the Queen of England and 25 DVDs to Prime Minister Gordon Brown are two of your biggest successes thus far. Who knows if you even took off the price tags?

It's shocking to look at the collection of schmucks you picked to help run this country. Timothy Geithner as Secretary of the Treasury! Are you serious? Here's a man-child admitting that the New York Fed failed miserably while under his leadership. He also conceded that massive policy errors were deeply responsible for the current economic crisis. In a sane society this tax cheat would be fortunate to run a Hot Dog on a Stick in Skokie, Illinois.

I can see why you appointed Hillary to Secretary of State. I know the two of you are Saul Alinsky disciples. Her senior thesis, "There is Only the Fight: An Analysis of the Alinsky Model" must have made her the frontrunner from day one. Her admiration for Planned Parenthood founder Margaret Sanger had to be icing on the cake. Clinton "admired her vision" and was "in awe of" the well documented bigot, racist, and eugenicist (she advocated for the elimination of the disabled, the downtrodden, and black children).

Clinton began her tenure by heading off to Russia for her first big overseas trip and gave Russian Foreign Minister, Sergey Lavrov that red button with the word "peregruzka" on it. Remember how she thought it was Russian for "reset," but instead it meant, "overcharged." Between this and Biden's *foot in mouth disease* I think we'd have better luck sending the Osbournes to do America's bidding.

Then you appoint former *Welcome Back Kotter* star,

DEAR OBAMA

Eric Holder as Attorney General. Here's a man who assisted former President Clinton in pardoning tax cheats and terrorists. He recently summed up his bias by calling Americans, "A nation of cowards" regarding race issues in the country. Obviously, he didn't see the irony of Americans electing the first African American president in the history of the United States. I have no doubt this is one activist who will have his nose buried in the Constitution.

I could go on and on, but I'll end by mentioning our fully alert Vice President, who I'm pretty sure is not even aware that he is Vice President! He's already a legend and it's only been a few months. The stories are endless, but today's gaffe credits the stimulus plan for funding a particular fire station—except that the station was actually funded under President George W. Bush.

I truly can't tell if these are our country's leaders or the old starting five who ran alongside Nicholson and Chief Bromden. I find it pathetic that not one of your top appointees has ever produced a product or service that the people of this country needed. You've saddled us with a melting pot of career politicians, academics, Socialists, Marxists, lobbyists, and bureaucrats. Well done sir, well done …

It is only a matter of time before you receive an Evite from Chris Matthews for a weekend getaway to the Pocono's.

One last thing: Gotcha! … APRIL FOOLS' DAY!

Sincerely kidding,
Chris

DEAR OBAMA

April 7, 2009

Dear Obama,

Do you know what one of the best things about liberalism is? There is no evil in the world! Once I became intellectually engaged with this enlightened generation and the "Coexist" supporters, the world miraculously became a peaceful place (with the exception of the US and its imperialism). It's a liberating mindset to see past and present rabble-rousers as nothing more than misunderstood. So-called evil tyrants or dictators are just human beings who tend to be a little more mischievous than others (a behavior easily cured by Ritalin, or running their fingers through Timothy Geithner's hair). In this utopia, Mussolini could have easily justified his actions by claiming, "At least I'm no Hitler."

This moral equivalency has the potential to achieve world peace far quicker and safer than any war or conflict. If George W. would have appreciated the fact that Saddam was just a son, father, husband, mentor (and probably a trial lawyer), we could have saved many lives. Saddam's stadium executions, beheadings, tortures, rape rooms, and mass graves were actually a part of a community outreach program. We, as an inferior and ignorant nation, had difficulty understanding the value of such things. In fact, Democrats can tell you that what transpires during a Republican National Convention is far more atrocious than anything that occurred during Hussein's regime (not our Hussein).

Nevertheless, such moral equivocation led seven

Democrats to Havana over the weekend. The "savant seven" praised Fidel Castro calling him warm and receptive during their "diplomatic mission." Bobby Rush was quoted as saying, "It was almost like listening to an old friend." He found Castro's home to be modest and his wife to be particularly hospitable.

It was clear that they were not there to negotiate with the Castro brothers the release of imprisoned human-rights advocates, dissidents, journalists, and prisoners of conscience, at least not on this trip. Their goal for this trip was to discuss reinstituting an open dialogue with Cuba, loosening the travel embargo, and to ask Fidel if he wears anything but jumpsuits.

I wasn't able to read over their entire itinerary, but I'm assuming they were able to visit with Óscar Elías Biscet, a doctor and follower of Martin Luther King Jr., serving twenty plus years for engaging in peaceful resistance. Even if they weren't able to find Biscet, it still appears to have been a very successful trip. How could it not be when Castro looks you in the eye and says, "How can we help? How can we help President Obama?"

Sincerely,
Chris

April 14, 2009

Dear Obama,

If you ask anyone close to me they will tell you two things:

one, I'm a planner, and two, I have excellent ideas. I bring this up because I'm already thinking about life for you after your presidency. I know it's early in your reign, but after you eliminate the 22nd Amendment and allow for multiple presidential terms, thirty years will have passed before you can say "Havana."

Here's what I'm thinking. We all know that your skills and expertise in managing a teleprompter are unprecedented. I think you should capitalize (sorry, wrong choice of words). I think you should profit (did it again). I think you should acquire fair and modest means at the government's discretion for this God-given ability. Since the teleprompter is now an iconic image, I was thinking you should present a pilot to MTV titled *Pimp My Teleprompter*. It would obviously be a spin off from the very successful show, *Pimp my Ride*. The basic format would be similar, with a few tweaks and surprises.

What you would do is travel around the country visiting deserving schools, town hall locations, etc., with teleprompters in need of repair or updating. Once the applicants and logistics are determined, you could take over from there. I'm sure with your years of experience you have plenty of creative and wacky ideas. I can already think of a few off the top of my head: diamond encrusted railings, original hammer and sickle prints on the belly of the prompter, adding hydraulics at the base of the stand, PlayStation adapter, you know, anything that might add a little bling and give new life to a "Tricked out Tele." If I come up with any more suggestions I will make sure to document them.

I watched the original *Raiders of the Lost Ark* the other

DEAR OBAMA

night. You know the famous opening scene where Indy is going to switch the sack of sand for the golden idol. I thought it would have been so cool if that whole scene were about Indy braving the jungles of South America in search of the Golden Teleprompter. I love the part where Indy is letting the sand fall through his fingers as he stares at the beautiful idol. If only he was staring at a priceless gold teleprompter. You wouldn't even have to change the script that much: "Give me the whip! Throw me the teleprompter and I'll give you the whip … no time to argue."

If Spielberg only knew then, what he knows now …

Sincerely,
Chris

"In the summer, because of the heat and high humidity, you could literally smell the tourist coming into the Capitol. It may be descriptive but it's true."

– Senate Majority Leader Harry Reid

April 22, 2009

Dear Obama,

The cover image of the latest *Washingtonian* has a picture of you shirtless and coming out of the ocean. There's just something very presidential about our Leader on the covers

DEAR OBAMA

of *The National Enquirer*, *People*, and *Star Magazine* wearing board shorts.

What a firestorm with Miss California. I'm sure you've been briefed about this serious domestic quagmire. As you know, Carrie Prejean is in a bunch of hot water for answering a question on gay marriage. As a Christian, she believes in traditional marriage between one man and one woman. Despite the fact that you, Vice President Biden, the State of California, and 70% of the nation agree with her, we all know the right answer to that question: not only should gay people be allowed to marry, but also be celebrated and given greater rights than hetero citizens. The ACLU has threatened her with a lawsuit on "thought discrimination," but nothing has been filed as of yet.

It finally hit me that Howard Dean is no longer in charge of the DNC. I'm sure going to miss that stable fellow. It's weird to think back to 2004 and how close he was to becoming president. It must be extremely disappointing to have your presidential aspirations derailed by a simple crazed outburst. I can only imagine the earful his aide received for screwing up his daily dose of medication.

Tim Kaine has wasted no time in filling his shoes. Members of his staff have already indicated that they are preparing for 2016. Mr. Kaine has hinted that they have their sights on Zig Ziglar as a potential candidate. He knows that he's a great speaker and motivator, and if we add some corruption, (nearly a billion dollars' worth), and a Chavez-backed media behind him, we'll have a winner.

DEAR OBAMA

But we don't have to worry about 2016 right now...

Sincerely,
Chris

April 29, 2009

Dear Obama,

We're not short on headlines these days. We have long-time liberal Arlen Specter leaving the Republican Party, the Swine Flu outbreak, the first 100 days of your presidency, and rare footage of Speaker Pelosi's face in its original state.

I'm counting on Homeland Security Secretary, Janet Napolitano to use the Swine Flu outbreak as a reason to quarantine conservatives. Not that you need an extra reason, but to me it just looks like a golden opportunity to implement Rahm Emanuel's strategy of "never letting a crisis go to waste." Conservatives are probably carriers of the host virus anyway.

I have to say I'm a little confused at all the media analysis hype of your first 100 days. It seems pointless and actually a bit comical to me that they're going to try and grade your performance—if they didn't already know. I hate to spoil it for any moron who's been living under a rock for the past three months, but let me sum it up for them in one word, "brilliant." In fact, I could have told you 100 days ago that your first 100 days were going to be brilliant. It's pretty simple folks ...

DEAR OBAMA

However, just for fun let's assume that I'm a crazy right-winged political pundit summarizing my 100-day report card of you. For no real reason, let's title it, "The Oxymoron President:"

- Appointed tax cheat Timothy Geithner to head the IRS.
- Appointed Leon Panetta, who has no intelligence experience, to head the Central Intelligence Agency.
- Increased spending by trillions when we're broke.
- Decreased spending on defense while our enemies, dictators, and any other of Sean Penn's allies are increasing military and defense spending.
- Appointed Harry Knox to the White House Advisory Council on Faith-Based Partnerships, someone who has strongly criticized the Pope, and has said the Knights of Columbus (a Catholic Men's Organization) was a group of "foot soldiers" in a "discredited army of oppression."
- Tried to appoint New Hampshire Senator Judd Gregg as Commerce Secretary, despite the fact that Gregg voted in favor of abolishing the Commerce Department in 1995.
- Talked about unilateral disarmament a day after Kim Jong Il sent a missile over Japan.
- Appointed Janet Napolitano as Homeland Security Secretary (a department specifically created after 9/11 to fight terrorism), who doesn't believe in using the word "terrorism."

DEAR OBAMA

- Has yet to offer any campaign-promised transparency, including no transparency on why there hasn't been any transparency.
- Appointed Ron Bloom "Car Czar," despite his lack of experience in the auto industry.

I know Barney Frank is not part of your administration, but I thought the following would be worth noting considering the theme. He recently declared that he is going after those responsible for the economic meltdown.

Bless his heart …

Sincerely,
Chris

May 6, 2009

Dear Obama,

Program details have just been unveiled regarding your federal budget for the fiscal year starting in October. The biggest headline is about you trimming roughly $17 billion from a $3.4 trillion budget. This 0.05% in cost cutting is exactly the kind of fiscal discipline the people have been begging for. In fact, your extreme frugality may appear to many as too ambitious. I've already heard frustration from some whom suggest that you might as well have slashed the entire $3,400,000,000,000.00.

DEAR OBAMA

In fairness to them, after severe penny-pinching, the numbers do look pretty meager. All you've left the spendthrifts in Washington is $3,383,000,000,000.00. How are they to better our lives on that kind of budget? However, you did make a strong, non-ironical statement explaining your motives: "We can no longer afford to spend as if deficits don't matter and waste is not a problem. We can no longer afford to leave the hard choices for the next budget, the next administration—or the next generation."

The only problem I've noticed so far is the request to double the tax law enforcement budget. The downside is that you run the risk of eventually depleting your own administration. Then again, you do have the executive order sitting in your holster.

I was also encouraged by your press conference when you took a strong stance against overseas tax shelters. I liked the "show and tell" format with current tax haven aficionado, Charlie Rangel by your side showing and telling. He was kind enough to use himself as an example of how tax shelters actually work. As a service to this country, he failed over the course of several years, to disclose $75,000 in rental income on his Dominican Republic Villa. Your praise for him at today's press conference was indeed warranted and informative. You disclosed his important role (along with others) of reining in those taking advantage of this loophole:

> The way to make American businesses competitive is not to let some citizens and businesses dodge their responsibility, while ordinary Americans pick up the

slack. Unfortunately, that's exactly what we're doing. These problems have been highlighted by Chairmen Charlie Rangel and Max Baucus, by leaders like Senator Carl Levin and Congressman Lloyd Doggett, and now is the time to finally do something about them.

I couldn't tell if Chairman Rangel was cuffed or not, but he appeared to be in good spirits. Either way, we are indeed fortunate to have him in charge of the House Ways and Means Committee, which by the way, is responsible for writing the country's tax laws.

What a crazy world . . .

Sincerely,
Chris

May 7, 2009

Dear Obama,

Eric Holder, our esteemed Attorney General, made a point today to say that your administration is not going to release the Gitmo prisoners into the US. Personally, I disagree with this decision, because I feel the "adopt-a-terrorist" program has unlimited potential.

It should be noted that if it weren't for you, we wouldn't even have room in our overcrowded prisons to even consider housing terrorists. By giving several jobs to tax cheats and others involved in criminal activity, you've eased the strain on our prison system. Attorney General Holder should thank you for giving him this option.

Wrapped up in this controversy is the issue of enhanced interrogations, or more specifically, waterboarding. Cleary this technique is torture and those responsible for conducting it on the 9/11 masterminds should be prosecuted under UN law. Why are we still debating this?

Last night I heard right-wing stooge, Ann Coulter attempt to make the case that waterboarding isn't even close to torture. Once again, she has to bring up abortion. She asked which is worse: water poured on your head for thirty seconds, or your head punctured, brains sucked out, limbs dismembered, and the remains vacuumed out? All right, Ms. Coulter, but what if the water happens to be cold, or there's no towel to dry off afterwards, or no Q-tips available to help get the water out of your ears?

Sincerely,
Chris

May 15, 2009

Dear Obama,

Torture and waterboarding continue to rule the media cycle. I recently wrote about my feelings on the subject. However, what I didn't mention is the impact it is having on our environment. Having lived in California my whole life, this is a sensitive subject for me. To Californians, water is a precious resource, but to the Bush administration, it was just another resource for Mengele's playbook. We've been dealing with water rationing and worrying about droughts for as long as I can remember. Do you know how much water is wasted on waterboarding? Where's the outrage?

Keeping terrorists comfortable might become the new civil rights issue of our time. Torturing them with water or loud music is both heinous and unacceptable, even for an imperialist nation. If we "have" to get terrorists to talk, why don't we just send them to Costco on a Sunday afternoon? After experiencing that joy for an hour or two they'll be begging to be waterboarded!

Sincerely,
Chris

May 19, 2009

Dear Obama,

It's a Special Election day in California. Most initiatives on the ballot are tax increase propositions. Since our state is in financial ruin we need to find additional means of raising revenues. Where better to get the funds than from the people themselves? I'm considering voting "Yes" on all the propositions, but it is a bit confusing to me. To begin with, I can't seem to grasp why California is in such bad shape. I don't mind that California has one of the highest state income taxes in the country. It just surprises me that with all that money coming in we still have double-digit unemployment, a $40 billion deficit, and businesses and families leaving the state in droves. Considering the state is completely run by progressives one would naturally conclude that we would be progressing/prospering.

Teachers' salaries in California are 35% higher than the national average. Yes, we're second to last in test scores, but we're not last. It just doesn't make sense. I guess the only logical conclusion is that it's not enough money. We need to raise more taxes and continue to pump more money into our educational system, state bureaucracies, eco-friendly programs, etc. It will eventually pay off … it has to.

It's like we live in a bizarro world, Mr. President. Up is down; good is bad and right is wrong. How is it that most states that are governed by progressives are doing horribly? When we look at these beloved progressive states like Michigan, Illinois, (your own state for goodness sake), New Jersey, Vermont, Oregon, Taxachussetts, New York, California, etc., we can see they're floundering in high unemployment, failing school systems, corruption, and massive amounts of debt.

Yet nearly all states run by conservatives are doing well. It drives me crazy that states like Texas, Indiana, Utah, Tennessee, Idaho, and the "Moose Killer's" state are doing fine considering the current economic conditions. Even Louisiana is showing signs of life after the state elected conservative Bobby Jindal to succeed liberal governor Kathleen Blanco.

I don't mean to sound like a downer, but it's all very frustrating for us Californians. It's hard to figure out when you have impeccable leaders such as Barbara Boxer, Henry

DEAR OBAMA

Waxman, Diane Feinstein, and Maxine Waters leading the way.

Sincerely,
Chris

May 21, 2009

Dear Obama,

I was on your website again and there was another text message exchange between Vice President Biden and Madeline Albright:

Biden: S.O.S.!!!
Albright: what's wrong joe?
Biden: i need your help fast!!
Albright: what is it? u r scaring me
Biden: i'm leaving in a cupl hours 4 lebanon 2 meet with pres. sleiman
Albright: and?
Biden: i need 2 borrow your travel neck pillow 4 the flight
Albright: that's the emergency?
Biden: not that I'm meeting sleiman, but the neck pillow
Albright: what happened 2 yours?
Biden: it popped when i rolled over on my last trip
Albright: it popped from rolling over?
Biden: i had a toothpick in my mouth

DEAR OBAMA

Albright: i'll get it 2 you
Biden: thanks, 1 more thing
Albright: what is it?
Biden: i want 2 bring a present 4 him
Albright: and?
Biden: well the pres. raised the bar on gift giving after the brown meeting
Albright: what r u thinking?
Biden: 26 DVDs, just kidding
Albright: u better b, u don't want 2 come off as more generous
Biden: any other ideas?
Albright: what about a bobblehead? they can b so captivating
Biden: and intriguing
Albright: do you still have the 1's i got u?
Biden: i'm looking at regis as we speak
Albright: did u ever find kathy lee?
Biden: nope, did kim jong il like the autographed jordan basketball?
Albright: absolutely!
Biden: i have an old autographed meadowlark lemon program
Albright: the globetrotter?
Biden: yes, except i spilled yoohoo on it a couple years ago
Albright: is it ruined?
Biden: not really, it now reads dowlark lem.
Albright: i don't think so jb.
Biden: i'll probably end up going with my first instinct
Albright: what?

DEAR OBAMA

Biden: guitar hero

Sincerely,
Chris

"I would hope that a wise Latina woman with the richness of her experiences would more often than not reach a better conclusion than a white male."

– Sonia Sotomayor (Supreme Court nominee)

May 26, 2009

Dear Obama,

You are officially the new "Sultan of Swat." Every time your office reaches a major decision or appointee you hit it out of the park. Today's nomination of Sonia Sotomayor to the Supreme Court is nothing less than a Grand Slam. I always knew you would appoint judicial activists, but to nominate one who has publicly stated it is truly inspiring.

In 2005, while addressing a group of law students at Duke University, Sotomayor said that the US Court of Appeals "is where policy is made." With your extensive constitutional law background, I'm sure this was all you needed to know about her. Thankfully, we are seeing more and more of this. It's common for judges to hand down policy rulings based purely on what makes them feel good. Who likes feeling uneasy anyway?

DEAR OBAMA

The one thing I find most exciting about this pick is something I'm sure you didn't even consider. By nominating a Hispanic woman you've not only stroked the Hispanic base, but the female voters as well. How lucky is that? You inadvertently get a political benefit out of this too.

Despite this historic nomination, you are just replacing one liberal for another. There's a good possibility you will have the opportunity to nominate at least two more judges during your first term. Ginsburg's health is failing and Stevens is closing in on 124 years. The only way I can see any real change is if Anthony Kennedy or a conservative judge retires. If I were you, I wouldn't wait for this. I would attempt what FDR, one of your heroes, tried to do. During his presidency, he was having trouble with the Supreme Court so he tried to add six additional judges. His goal was to have a total of fifteen judges instead of nine on the bench. Obviously, he wasn't successful, but then again he didn't have your charisma or Toastmaster skills.

The only damper in the news lately is the fallout of North Korea and its nuclear bomb test over the weekend. I'm surprised that the strong words you and the UN have been saying to Pyongyang haven't been more effective. Personally, I would have taken it a step further and demanded he immediately limit all missile and nuclear testing to no more than five demonstrations per week. I would give in to six if concessions were met regarding Kim Jong Il's hair.

By the way, I checked, and Mr. Il does NOT have a Facebook account yet. I don't know who started this rumor, but I want to make it clear that whoever made that claim is either mistaken or flat out lying. You're going to have to find an alternative medium for engaging in diplomatic negotiations with Mr. Il.

Sincerely,
Chris

> *"Hey, Obama has just nationalized nothing more and nothing less than General Motors. Comrade Obama! ... Fidel, careful or we are going to end up to his right."*
>
> *– Hugo Chavez*

June 2, 2009

Dear Obama,

I'm on the way out the door, but I wanted to quickly share my excitement regarding your "glowing" endorsement from *Pravda*, Russia's leading newspaper. On May 30th they were quoted as saying, "America's descent into Marxism is happening with breathtaking speed." I'm surprised our own state run media hasn't picked up on this yet, but in their defense they don't have Russia's long history. Russians have had much more experience with this ideology, and would no doubt be able to spot it well before the average American.

Most likely what solidified Pravda's assessment was your recent government seizure of General Motors forcing it into bankruptcy. It's basic Marx strategery (I can't help it) 101. Those who've studied history, or who are not under the influence, can see this as clear as day. It's inevitable that you will add other corporations to your collection. It's just a matter of whom, when, and for how many euros.

For the record, I would like to state that I did not find it in poor taste to have a date night with Michelle a day after GM declared bankruptcy. The cost to the average taxpayer of flying two airplanes and three helicopters to New York for dinner and a Broadway show is perfectly acceptable and well deserved considering the pressure you're under. I don't think the people understand how stressful hostile takeovers of corporations can be.

On a separate note, I felt the Chinese were incredibly disrespectful to Timmy Geithner during his recent visit to Shanghai. Most of us heard about the economic students laughing at him as he assured them that their country's investment in the dollar was safe (kind of a backhanded slap at you and your policies).

However, a second mocking was largely unreported, but equally outrageous. When Mr. Geithner was initially introduced as the United States Secretary of Treasury, all the students laughed in disbelief. They were convinced he was just an American student, part of an international school field trip. Most had seen him earlier in the day taking in the sites wearing skinny jeans, a hoodie and a Jonas Brothers backpack.

They can laugh and mock all they want, but who is stuck with $2 trillion in worthless US Treasuries?

DEAR OBAMA

Psych!

Sincerely,
Chris

June 6, 2009

Dear Obama,

The Romanov's have got nothing on you. Your most recent "Czar" announcement now puts around twenty "Czars" in your administration (that we know). The Romanov Dynasty capped out at eighteen, the most in history to that point. You've definitely taken advantage of a loophole that past presidents deemed questionable or Stalinesque.

Critics have been unhinged in their opposition to all this. They have yet to realize that your "Czar Program" is nothing more than a super Kiwanis club. I don't see what the big deal is. All they offer you is unfettered executive power, in exchange for zero accountability and carte blanche to do whatever they want. Personally, I feel they get the short end of the stick. The least we can do is make certain they dodge the annoying confirmation process ... oh wait, they do.

Breaking the Romanov record is certainly worthy of acknowledgement, but I don't know if we can credit you with this last "Czar" coronation. The main reason is because the EPA handed it down. The Environmental Protection Agency chose Cameron Davis to head the cleanup of the Great Lakes. Mr. Davis, who has been embedded in Chicago politics for years, will have $20 billion at his disposal. Experts believe only a nominal amount, maybe $10 billion, will be funneled to political cronies in Illinois and Michigan.

Prior to Mr. Davis, you introduced Kenneth Feinberg as the country's new "Pay Czar," or "special master for compensation." The duties of this non-fascist position will be to keep tabs on executive salaries, mainly CEOs and other corporate executives. I'm assuming the oversight will be limited to those corporate types. I see no use for this program outside of corporate America. We all know that other industries have perfectly suitable salaries. Hollywood producers, directors, actors, and other A-listers are certainly reasonably compensated. This goes too for professional athletes, network executives, former Vice Presidents and global warming advocates, many in the music industry, where hip-hop moguls are living paycheck to paycheck.

You also did this country a huge favor by creating a "Cyber Czar" for internet security. Although I know you are much too clever to not have already been monitoring your critics, opponents, and other dissidents via the internet.

Another "Czar" rumored to be in the pipeline is "MTV Czar." The objective of this position will be to make sure the popular cable station continues to steer our youth towards promiscuity and substance abuse, with the ultimate goal of complete degeneracy.

Lastly, "Fist Bump Czar" has been temporarily shelved due to lack of qualified applicants. Aides close to you have confirmed that you are frustrated about not filling the position. This has prompted rumors that you may have no choice but to tap yourself for this position. Whoever ends up landing the job will be responsible for overseeing the public's proper use of this highly sophisticated, yet often bungled expression of coolness.

Shizzle ...

Sincerely,
Chris

June 10, 2009

Dear Obama,

I've had a few days to digest last week's unemployment numbers, and I came up with two conclusions. One, the numbers are not as bad they appear, and two, your critics suck. Just once I'd like to see conservatives offer a sliver of bipartisanship and support you no matter how bad the news is.

We all understand that 9.4% unemployment is a little higher than what you forecasted a few months back during the stimulus push. You stated with certainty that if the stimulus bill were passed, unemployment would not exceed 8%. In hindsight, this was more of a generalization.

This 9.4% that was carelessly thrown out by the US Bureau of Labor Statistics does not account for many non-traditional jobs. This includes selling goods and services on eBay and Craigslist, bartering, and one of the more underrated and unique careers, Independent Botanical Sales

DEAR OBAMA

Representatives specializing in the distribution of herbal fun plants (most prevalent in the area of Humboldt and Eureka, California). Although considered a "green" job, it's not as eco-friendly as many would have you believe. After all, the product is generally distributed in environmentally destructive plastic baggies.

It's difficult to gauge exactly how many citizens or non-citizens are self-employed. Unfortunately for you, these jobs are lost in an untraceable abyss. How many little kids do you see selling lemonade on street corners? No doubt they are undocumented rogue capitalists taking advantage of the system. If they're going to steal from the government, the least we can do is incorporate their labor into the numbers.

My point is that these gainfully employed Americans need to be factored in the overall unemployment data. Yes, it would be difficult to accurately quantify their contribution, but just get creative. I am certain that with your crack economic team you could get that unemployment number down to wherever you think is reasonable. Remember you're dealing with a public that has bought into your "saved and created jobs" mantra.

Sincerely,
Chris

DEAR OBAMA

June 11, 2009

Dear Obama,

I would like to take this moment to say congratulations to the Los Angeles Lakers. They defeated the Orlando Magic in only five games to win the NBA Championship. The Lakers, as you may or may not know, are my favorite team. They have been since I was a little kid. Considering you are a Chicagoan, I assume you are a Chicago Bulls fan.

This particular win for the Lakers was not only impressive, but it has historical implications. Their coach, Phil Jackson, passed Boston Celtic legend, Red Auerbach for the most titles (ten) won by a coach. However, it should be noted that three of the ten titles have an asterisk, as they were won during W's presidency.

Time will tell if this record will officially stand and whether the Hall of Fame will recognize it. I would like to think so, but rumors are swirling that George Mitchell has been tapped again to lead another money draining, insomnia-curing special investigation into the legitimacy of all major sports achievements during George W. Bush's presidency. Nevertheless, congratulations to Coach Jackson and especially Kobe Bryant, for their first post-W NBA title.

Sincerely,
Chris

DEAR OBAMA

June 12, 2009

Dear Obama,

My son graduated from kindergarten today. You should have seen him. He was so proud standing up on stage in his little cap and gown. I know it's just kindergarten, but I'm sure you know as a parent that every milestone in your child's life is worthy of celebration. After the ceremony, we all met for dinner and dessert. We told family members not to give gifts, but if they felt inclined to give money towards his college education, we'd appreciate it in Euros or the Chinese Yuan.

Next school year stands to be a very exciting one. He is now at the prime age for indoctrination so we're hoping the school will start right away. We may be biased, but we believe our son is highly intelligent and would have no trouble tackling advanced subjects. We think he would excel in Basic Philosophy contemplating thought provoking questions such as: if Keith Olbermann hosted a TV show on cable and no one tuned in, would he still make a sound? If Chris Dodd put Wite-Out in his hair, would you be able to tell? And, if John Kerry and Al Gore spoke simultaneously, would the earth slip into a permanent state of hibernation? I'm not saying they should delve straight into the works of Kierkegaard or Spinoza, but I don't think analyzing Nietzsche's claim that "God is dead" would be too much for him. He's old enough to understand full well that your existence alone refutes this claim.

I'm also very excited about the prospect of introducing him to science. I think it's important for kids to learn at a young age that you can actually tweak science to fit your agenda. Science used to be defined as: "a systematic knowledge base or prescriptive practice resulting in infallible outcomes." For example, the sun is 93 million miles away from earth whether you run the formula backwards or forwards. Now, all you need to do is simply *claim* a "consensus" among "experts, regardless if there is an irrefutable conclusion.

This new form of "progressive science" includes such hot button issues as global warming, stem cell research, and abortion. If you listen to the new breed of "scientists," they will rightfully argue that the "old" science, rooted in fact, must take a back seat to a more tolerant view of science (i.e. non-discriminatory formulas, affirmative outcomes, etc.) So it is important that my son get a head start on the inner workings of scientific manipulation.

Sincerely,
Chris

P.S. I checked next year's curriculum and "Gender Reassignment Surgery: Is It For You?" is not offered in the first semester . . .oh well.

June 14, 2009

Dear Obama,

Let us celebrate. On this date in 1928 the great Ernesto "Che" Guevara was born. As you can imagine, I've become a huge fan of his. I also know that I am not alone in my admiration. That is why I believe it is time that we start honoring this man's birthday.

As it stands, we only have a couple days a year when we get to celebrate honor and excellence. Yes, we have Martin Luther King, Jr. Day and a few presidential birthdays, but it's time we added one more. Forget American hacks such as Booker T. Washington, Dwight Eisenhower, and Frederick Douglass. Let's take advantage of the iconic status of Guevara that Hollywood and the far left have been marketing for years.

Last year's release of Steven Soderbergh's "Che" should be considered a great resource and learning tool regarding Guevara and his overall contribution to the world. For those yet to see the film, this "Biopic" should clear up any misunderstandings about Guevara. Although a humble man, he once bragged, "We execute from revolutionary conviction," and "Judicial evidence is an archaic bourgeois detail."

Of course with any movie you're not going to be able to cover everything. It's clear Soderbergh didn't have enough room in the film to acknowledge the fact that in Cuba he was the chief executioner and supported a regime that outlawed elections and private property. His regime also stole the savings and property of millions leaving nearly a quarter of the population as refugees. Among the other highlights that Soderbergh's editing team begrudgingly left out of the film was the forced labor camps, the torture and prison camps, and the abolishment of habeas corpus, which he and Fidel accomplished shortly after taking power.

Che the "Freedom Fighter" also cherished his execution

yard "La Cabaña." This is where he oversaw numerous summary executions. At one point he even removed a wall so he could see the actual firing squad. Perhaps a ghoulish decision in the eyes of some, but maybe he was nothing more than a micromanager.

Now I understand this isn't your traditional resume and that he's not an American citizen, but should that be grounds to disqualify him from having his birthday recognized as a federal holiday? All I'm suggesting, Mr. President, is that we at least consider acknowledging the month of June as "La Cabaña" month to commemorate the murderous rampage he led in 1959. I know the word murderous generally has a negative connotation, but in this context we're only talking about "eliminating" Christians, intellectuals, artists, homosexuals, dissidents, and children.

No doubt Marx inspired his "dreams of a classless society, a society that isn't built on the profit motive." It's no wonder I, and many others, were not shocked to see a Che Guevara flag draped on the walls of your Houston office during the campaign.

He is also the inspiration behind the upcoming documentary about Senate Majority leader Harry Reid and Speaker of the House Nancy Pelosi. *The Motorcade Diaries* is an inspiring look at the two political icons as they travel the country in search of truth, honor, and Thorazine. One of the more emotional moments of the film is when Reid discovers himself by a creek off the highway in Billings, Montana. This film is not yet rated.

Sincerely,
Chris

DEAR OBAMA

June 17, 2009

Dear Obama,

Your strong principled stance on the disputed Iranian elections confirms our suspicions that you are a natural leader. It took no more than a minute or two in an unscripted moment for you to draw the proverbial "line in the sand" by stating you have "deep concerns" regarding the election, but that "it is not productive, given the history of US-Iranian relations, to be seen as meddling." Since you demonstrated such forceful rhetoric you do run the risk of inadvertently appointing yourself as "Conviction Czar."

Every time you speak in that slow, intellectual, "uh" kind of way, you prove again that you are the thoughtful academic we voted for, as opposed to a crafty politician with a dubious answer.

Continuing with your transparency promise, early reports confirmed that the White House denied requests by a non-partisan watchdog group for the names of recent White House visitors. Your administration argues that though a federal judge ruled that these records should be made public, a president has no obligation to reveal which White House visitors influence his policy decisions. Don't worry – your credibility is not at risk just because we can't see the names of Sean Penn, Noam Chomsky, and Lady Gaga.

We know America's staunchest supporter, George Soros, has a standing invitation to 1600 Pennsylvania Ave., and why shouldn't he? Mr. Soros made his name by bringing down the Bank of England in 1992 and destroying

Thailand and Indonesia's economies in 1997. I'm sure he has no desire to bring down the dollar, or America, since he was quoted saying, "The main obstacle to a stable and just world order is the United States."

I understand that you are indebted to this man both personally and financially. He was such a huge asset to your campaign as he contributed millions of unreported foreign campaign donations. As John McCain was documenting every red cent, this lovable Hungarian was funneling money to you from different resources all over the world. Who cares that you received $200 million in untraceable donations?

Nevertheless, I'm sure his weekly visit is centered on, "You owe me," and "I want a return on my "investment." Whether it's legalizing marijuana, prostitution, or bringing down capitalism, I expect his voice to have more clout than others. It doesn't take a genius to figure out why he is so beloved by the left. It is also no wonder that he is the leading candidate for UN Ambassador to Middle Earth.

Lastly, I must vent my outrage over the accusations that Senator Dick Durbin (D-IL) sold stock and mutual fund holdings in 2007, the day after meeting with former Secretary Treasurer Hank Paulson. First of all, I find it hard to believe that any politician from or even near the vicinity of Chicago could have such low moral integrity. Secondly, I just don't buy it. Durbin has a long distinguished track record of critical thinking, intimate knowledge of Blagojevich's intent on selling your Senate seat, and comparing American servicemen to Nazis, the Soviet Gulags, and the Khmer Rouge.

DEAR OBAMA

His "inner jackass" filtering system has yet to fail him, so why would it now? . . .

Sincerely,
Chris

June 23, 2009

Dear Obama,

It's my birthday today—thirty-eight years young. In fact, I would say I pretty much feel and look the exact same way as I did ten years ago, aside from unprecedented hair loss and an extra chin.

Wish you were here ...

Sincerely,
Chris

June 24, 2009

Dear Obama,

I just completed another round of extensive research on all past presidents and their accomplishments during the week of Quebec's St. Jean Baptiste Day. This is a silly question, but whom do you think ended up being the most successful president? B.O. baby! These comparisons aren't even competitive anymore. How could they be when the sitting president kills a fly with his bare hands during a live interview (leaving the media in awe)? The speed and concentration alone would have made Mr. Miyagi proud ... chopsticks, schmopsticks.

Despite your critics, your Zen diplomacy has already proven to be very successful. We've longed for a leader to usher in this new style of progressive foreign diplomacy. Nothing puts fear in the hearts of tyrannical maniacs like the deafening silence from the world's superpower. Imagine the horror on Kim Jong Il's face when you responded by playing eighteen holes after North Korea went public with its plan to fire a missile towards Hawaii. The same could be said for Iran. As its people protested in defiance over a fraudulent election, you stood by those risking their lives in the streets by making it clear to the world that we are not going to "meddle" in Iran's affairs.

What many of your detractors don't understand is that based on empirical evidence, you very well could be a "Jedi Knight" planning to use the "force" with many of these dictators. Similar to when Obi-Wan Kenobi used the Jedi mind trick on the storm troopers in the original *Star Wars*: "These aren't the droids you're looking for. He can go about his business. Move along ..."

It's conceivable you plan on taking this mystical approach to diplomacy with Mahmoud Ahmadinejad when you meet him face to face (without preconditions). Your strategy regarding Israel might go something like this: "These aren't the Jews you're looking for. They can go about their business. Move along ... you may continue with your peaceful desire for nuclear proliferation." And like that, the Middle East problem is solved. We've seen firsthand the power of your words and how they can fool the weak-minded.

History is keeping score:

Silence/Jedi mind trick: 2
Peace through strength: 0

Sincerely,
Chris

June 27, 2009

Dear Obama,

That was a close one ... your sneaky firing of Inspector General Gerald Walpin could not have come at a better time. It's been confirmed that he was very close to spilling the beans on an investigation into the misuse of federal grant money by the current mayor of Sacramento, former NBA great Kevin Johnson. Apparently Johnson, a staunch supporter of yours, was using federal funds intended for a nonprofit organization for personal and political purposes. Thankfully, the unrest in Iran, the socialized medicine debate, North Korea's plan to launch a missile at Hawaii, and *Jon & Kate Plus 8*'s messy divorce has overshadowed your political housekeeping.

When Mr. Walpin was asked to investigate reports of irregularities at St. Hope (Johnson's nonprofit group in

California), he discovered that grant money was being used illegally. The funds were intended for tutoring students, theater and arts programs, and redevelopment. Instead, they were being used to politically intervene in a local school election, bump up pay for staffers, and pay for personal services, including detailing his car.

Ironically, the job of an Inspector General is non-political and is protected to a certain degree. Your administration rightfully sidestepped the law, which usually requires the President to give Congress thirty days' notice, plus the reason for dismissing an IG. Sadly, people are still ignorant and don't know how to play Chicago-style politics. $850,000 of fraud in the Windy City is equivalent to stealing a box of Milk Duds from a convenience store.

Predictably, Republicans and even some Democrats balked at the fact that you gave Mr. Walpin, a W. appointee, only one hour to resign or be fired. You also gave him no immediate cause for his termination. Your henchman later clarified your reasons by saying he was, "confused and disoriented." It was a perfectly credible, not to mention detailed explanation. With precedent now set, one wonders the fate of Vice President Biden.

For the record, I happen to agree with those who say it took "political courage" to fire Mr. Walpin. By not terminating him sooner, you risked letting this investigation potentially take down a fierce supporter of yours and even implicate your own administration. This was a little out of character for you; normally, you tend to get such things nipped in the bud. At least it's over. The last thing Washington needs is some brown-nosing, do-gooder honorably performing his duties.

DEAR OBAMA

I always hated those kids in school. They made everyone else look bad...

Sincerely,
Chris

> "We need to do a lot more to reverse the global trend towards fatness. It is a key factor in the battle to reduce carbon emissions and slow climate change."
>
> – Dr. Phil Edwards, London School of Hygiene and Tropical Medicine

June 29, 2009

Dear Obama,

I've had a few days to let this global warming bill sink in. As an "honorary scientist," you clearly displayed your expertise when you claimed, "Carbon dioxide contaminates the water we drink and pollutes the air we breathe." Incredibly well said. While the nitpickers will point out the fallacy in that statement, the rest of us will certainly feel better about ourselves. It's one of those claims that if you say it enough times it starts to sound better and better and truer and truer.

Cap and trade is clearly our best shot at bringing our economy down to the standard of the third, if not the fourth world. We have a very small window and have to ram this bill through as the skeptics continue to be weary. Strangely, the other side has been using statistics and logic to present their opposing view. Personally, I don't know how someone can watch you promote this hopium-laced bill and not see the advantages.

I thought it was smart having Rahm Emanuel and Speaker Pelosi out there "encouraging" hesitant members of Congress. I'm sure many of them thought it was odd that baseball bats and *Goodfellas* DVDs were sent to their offices, but who am I to say? I'm assuming you saved one of these care packages for EPA analyst Alan Carlin. He recently published a report questioning the science behind global warming. Your administration dismissed this fringe character, and his 97-page pile of garbage.

What haven't been dismissed are the recent reports "experts" submitted which substantiate claims that both cow flatulence and fat people are contributing to this "inconvenient truth." Scientists maintain that, "the slow digestive system of cows designates them a leading producer of methane, a potent greenhouse gas that receives far less social awareness than CO_2." As for the obese, well, the more they eat, the more food production, which then causes more CO_2 emissions, thus warming the planet. Dr. Phil Edwards, of the London School of Hygiene and Tropical Medicine, adds, "Moving about in a heavy body is like driving in a gas guzzler." An obese person emits a ton more climate-warming carbon dioxide than a skinny person which according to the World Health Organization means an extra billion tons of CO_2.

DEAR OBAMA

I'm not really one for eugenics, but if "science" says the tubbies have to go to save the earth, well ...

Sincerely,
Chris

July 1, 2009

Dear Obama,

There are some days when certain events make me proud and honored to be an American. Today is one of those days. Al Franken "officially" became a member of the United States Senate. The Minnesota Supreme Court handed to Franken—who oddly resembles an obscene phone call—a unanimous legal victory over Norm Coleman. I know it's been a long, drawn out process, but let me just say, congratulations Mr. Franken ... excuse me, Senator Franken.

Sincerely,
Chris

July 7, 2009

Dear Obama,

What a weekend. We decided to extend the Fourth of July holiday into a five-day mini-vacation. Some friends joined us as we traveled north to central California. We stayed in a quaint town that offers great eateries, numerous stores and specialty shops, surrounding wineries, and a beautiful beach community only ten minutes away.

As you would expect, I spent much of my time at the beach. I can't remember the last time I felt so relaxed. The peaceful surroundings were physically and spiritually rejuvenating. I felt fortunate that I had extra personal time to re-connect with you. My faith in you is attacked daily from the deceitful Right. However, the picturesque settings made it easy to forget the worries of the world and focus more on the brilliance of your leadership. I know this may sound strange, but for a brief moment I swear I saw an angelic image of a teleprompter hovering in the crystal blue sky.

Needless to say, it was very nice to get away from the hustle and bustle of everyday life. We were without a TV, which I'm proud to report I did not miss. However, I did have limited access to the internet allowing me some connection to the outside world, but really, what was I missing: Al Gore comparing global warming to the fight against the Nazis, Biden making another gaffe ("we misread the economy"), John Murtha defending another ethics probe, or you considering another "Czar" (a "Federal Insurance Czar"). Given the pattern here, I'll assume John Kerry undermined the troops again.

The only news that did surprise me over the weekend was hearing that Sarah Palin is stepping down as Governor of Alaska. I guess I shouldn't be that shocked. It was only a matter of time before this quitter succumbed to the pressure of the national spotlight. The hilarious part is that she thinks she can be president. Yet, if she can't take frivolous accusations, bogus ethics lawsuits, continual defamation of character, hit pieces against her and her children, and creepy innuendos from liberal pundits, then how can we expect her to stand up against our own allies, stand strong with the world's dictators, and bankrupt the country?

There are a lot of theories out there on why she did this. The most obvious one of course is that she is preparing for 2012. I don't really see how she can pull it off though. Her only support comes from the extreme hick segment of the Republican Party. She gets no support from moderates or independents, and definitely not from liberals. I suppose her only chance of garnering support from the Left would be to pose for *Playboy* or get busted for growing weed in her basement.

Sincerely,
Chris

P.S. I'm a little confused about Biden's comment regarding your administration misreading the economy. From day one you all declared that this is the worst economy since the Great Depression. Just wondering …

P.P.S. Never mind, I see that you clarified Biden's remark by asserting that you didn't misread the economy, but simply had "incomplete information."

DEAR OBAMA

July 10, 2009

Dear Obama,

"From Russia with Love ... and Peaceniks." That's one way I would summarize your work this week in Moscow when you unilaterally disarmed 1/3 of America's biggest deterrent and insurance policy—our nuclear weapons arsenal.

As the media allocated every possible electrical current to cover Michael Jackson's funeral, you were covertly inking deals with the always-trustworthy Russians. The best part of all was that you were able to ratify the Strategic Arms Reduction Treaty (START) while bypassing the Senate all together! Even though you hold sixty Senate seats in Congress, you decided to focus on the bigger picture. That's what I admire about you, you're always thinking ahead. Even though you have this congressional advantage, you're obviously setting a precedent for future cases.

White House Coordinator for Weapons of Mass Destruction, Security and Arms Control (and any other words that might make him sound important), Gary Samore said, "One option is that both sides could agree to continue the inspections by executive agreement; that would work on our side. On the Russian side, as I understand it, that would require Duma approval." It's a fine testament to the progress we've made in this country when Russia now has more checks and balances than the US.

There will always be some geeky, bookworm constitutionalist who will reference Article II, Section 2 of the US Constitution that states, "He shall have Power, by and with the Advice and Consent of the Senate, to make Treaties, provided two thirds of the Senators present concur." As a Constitutional Law Professor you know full well that this pesky document is more of a nuisance than a firm foundation. I'm just glad you're crafty enough to circumvent the legalities of it—as long as it's for the betterment of the people.

I remember back in March 2007 when you proudly referred to yourself as a "Constitutional Law Professor" and went on to say, "which means unlike the current President I actually respect the Constitution." You said this despite knowing that you were not tenured, had adjunct status, and your formal title was "Senior Lecturer." Frankly I, and the rest of us, don't care about that factual minutia. We just like referring to you as a "Constitutional Law Professor." It sounds so distinguished.

In case I don't get a chance to write to you, good luck with the start of Sonia Sotomayor's Supreme Court hearings next week. I sure hope she gets confirmed. I know she doesn't quite have the credentials of Ruth Bader Ginsburg, but then again who does?

Sincerely,
Chris

P.S. I heard Hugo was jealous when he saw you shake hands and exchange pleasantries with US admirer Muammar Gaddafi. I anticipate a fight brewing between the two comrades as they try to court BFF status with the coolest kid in the proverbial Red Square.

DEAR OBAMA

July 14, 2009

Dear Obama,

"Officials to probe color-coded terror alert system." If anyone out there still has doubts about the priorities of your administration, look no further than this gem. Homeland Security Secretary Janet Napolitano has apparently appointed a task force to analyze our current alert system. Her electrifying statement went as follows, "My goal is simple: to have the most effective system in place to inform the American people about threats to our country." Stop the press, why don't you …

The seventeen-member task force will be responsible for determining if a different terror alert system would ultimately be more effective. A few members of the group have already voiced their professional opinion that the color-coded approach is an antiquated system.

After their own internal analysis, they concluded that using shapes would actually be ideal for this type of warning system. They feel identifying shapes during a crisis situation might be fun and alleviate some of the stress that comes with an impending terrorist attack. They also made a point to condemn the current system because it discriminates against people who are colorblind.

Although as perfect as this new system sounds, it does have its drawbacks. Let's say for argument sake that around thirty to forty percent of the people in this country can recognize a circle, a square, and possibly even a triangle. But, after that, depending on the severity of the attack, the system would have to incorporate advanced shapes such as trapezoids, rhombuses— and heaven forbid—a hexagon. I'm sorry but that might be way too confusing and would likely create a panic, if there wasn't one already.

What you could do is switch gears and eliminate the alert system all together and go with a "comprehensive" reactive alert system. Wait for the attack, at which point you would immediately apologize to the group responsible for any grievances. Then first responders could assess the damage reporting any and all findings to Homeland Security. Secretary Napolitano could then analyze the information and release a proper post-threat level to the public with pinpoint accuracy.

All I know is that Ms. Napolitano continues to shine as the mastermind of America's national security. I confess ignorance regarding my initial reservations about her. She certainly has proven to the American people that she is up to the task. If I were a Vet, a Tea Party member, a pro-lifer or basically any other moderate/conservative in the country, I would grow eyes in the back of my head. Remember back on April 7th when DHS sent a nine-page warning memo to law enforcement offices across the country titled, "Rightwing Extremism: Current Economic and Political Climate Fueling Resurgence in Radicalization and Recruitment." With priorities such as this, and playing Mad Libs with terror related definitions, one wonders how long before Al Qaeda raises the white flag.

Sincerely,
Chris

DEAR OBAMA

July 17, 2009

Dear Obama,

It appears that the Sonia Sotomayor hearings are nearing the end and she will no doubt be confirmed. By the way, are you a *Scooby-Doo* fan? Every time I watch one of these Supreme Court confirmations, Senator Chuck Schumer (D-NY) makes me think of *Scooby-Doo*. He reminds me of the creepy guy who gets caught at the end of every show. When I say creepy, I just mean in that stalking, restraining-order kind of way. I keep waiting for him to pull off his mask and reveal his true identity. After the room gasps in shock, he angrily admits, "Yes it was me, and I would have gotten away with destroying the foundation of this country, if it wasn't for these meddling citizens."

For the record, I am a big fan of *Scooby-Doo*—the original one—not the lame episodes with Scrappy-Doo and his cousin Scooby-Dum . . .

Sincerely,
Chris

July 22, 2009

Dear Obama,

Bummer about your health care plan. I know there's a long way to go still, but man, there are some heartless people in this country. Obviously, the folks have yet to see Michael

Moore's compelling health care crockumentary *Sicko*. This is the film where Mr. Moore gives a behind-the-scenes look at one of the world's only countries to provide its citizens a "gold standard" in health care. This country of course is Cuba.

After viewing the film, one can only conclude that Cuba has the ideal model for high-quality, cost-effective health care. Even skeptics have little to criticize as its model was endlessly scrutinized and eventually validated by health "experts" (Moore's own production crew—various key grips, gaffers, and ultimately by the perfect health specimen himself).

My only advice for back here at home is to continue with the Alinsky principles. I promise that you will eventually wear them down, or they will just have to get used to their lack of kneecaps.

I also like how you met with the head of the Congressional Budget Office (CBO) John Elmendorf. This stunt was a little bold, even for you. It is unprecedented for a president to meet with the apolitical head, but it needed to be done. He and his group has definitely become a nuisance during this process. I don't know what you said or which family members of his are now in danger, but I'm expecting future budgets and cost analyses out of his office to be much different.

It's in uncertain times like this that I find comfort in the fact that you have stayed true to yourself. You have stuck to your guns, despite an unprecedented barrage of hatred towards you and your Castroite colleagues in Congress. Recent comments by Sam Webb, the National Chair of the Communist Party USA (CPUSA), have also reassured my

DEAR OBAMA

faith in you and the "cause." Here are a few quotes from him: "The new conditions of struggle are possible only—and I want to emphasize only—because we elected President Obama and a Congress with pronounced progressive and center currents." He's also a pragmatist: "Let's be aware that [Obama] has to keep a coalition together for his long-term as well as immediate legislative agenda. Let's give President Obama some space to change and to respond to pressures from below."

The former me would have despaired and downed a fifth of Jack Daniels after reading such an endorsement. Instead, I think I will celebrate with a shot of Stolichnaya.

Na zdorovia . . .

With Redness,
Chris

> *"I am sick of people who say that if you debate and disagree with this administration somehow you're not patriotic. We should stand up and say we are Americans and we have a right to debate and disagree with any administration." [shrieking]*
>
> *– Hillary Clinton, 2006*

DEAR OBAMA

August 6, 2009

Dear Obama,

How low will the GOP go? The stories I'm reading about "angry mobs" planted by the Republicans to disrupt local town hall meetings is outrageous, if not traitorous. The footage I've seen shows several individuals (many of them resembling Blanche and her sidekicks from *Golden Girls*) expressing concern over your proposed demolition of our health care system. In one shocking moment, a citizen even raised her hand a few inches higher in an effort to emphasize a point. If this was not an act of aggression, it was at least a "sieg heil."

    I have to keep reminding myself that it's now Healthcare "Insurance" Reform, the new phrase that your internal polling is telling you to use. How can you demonize that? You can't. We needed a villain, so I was happy to hear Speaker Pelosi say last week regarding the insurance companies: "Of course they've been immoral all along in how they have treated the people that they insure. They are the villains. They have been part of the problem in a major way."

Sincerely,
Chris

DEAR OBAMA

August 10, 2009

Dear Obama,

Not that it was a surprise, or that it needs to be said, but awesome speech on health care last night. Our praise for you after every major speech probably gets redundant, but if I may quote Vince Vaughn from the movie *Swingers*, "You're so money you don't even know you're money." Although in your case, maybe it should be, "You're so euro you don't even know you're euro."

The one thing that frustrates me when you deliver these historic speeches is that you always sound like a conservative. Last night I heard phrases such as "rugged individualism" and "self-reliance." It must pain you to know that the country is far more conservative than liberal and that you have to talk like a Republican to appear moderate. Don't worry, one day soon it won't be so politically incorrect to talk and act like a pure Marxist.

On the other hand, something I found admirable about your speech, as with all of them, is how blatantly obvious it is that you love America. Aside from the time you spent trashing our health care system and accusing it of murder, the other three minutes were as inspirational as any I've seen. It brought me back to your campaign when you stumped across the country touting how great America is, yet you wanted to "fundamentally change the US." This was a perfectly rational statement. When you love something and think it is great, the first thing you want to do is change it.

Naturally, your speech was marred with controversy.

DEAR OBAMA

South Carolina Congressman and Far Reich stooge Joe Wilson had the unmitigated gall to shout "You lie!" after you made a clear and concise statement deceiving the American people about health care coverage for illegal aliens. I know he called you immediately after the speech and apologized profusely, but I sure hope you explained to him that's not how subordinates are to behave. Whatever, it's done. Just promise me this coward has moved to the front of the labor-camp line.

On a side note, I find it ironic that the Left had no problem when Joe Biden would fire spit wads at President Bush during his major addresses. It was also perfectly acceptable for an Iraqi to throw a shoe at President Bush during one of his speeches. In fact, many thought it was hilarious and wished the guy had worn a bigger shoe. For the record, I did think it was funny, and I too wished he had been wearing Timberlands.

Sincerely,
Chris

August 13, 2009

Dear Obama,

I'm getting a vasectomy tomorrow. I wasn't too worried about it until the last few days. I'm sad to say my mind has fallen prey to the "what if" scenarios. What if we decide a year down the road we want another child? What if the procedure goes badly and I get a horrible infection? What if they get the medical records mixed up and they think I'm an amputee case? Sorry, that one makes me wince.

I know this is normal, but I still can't keep from letting these thoughts enter my mind. It's consumed my thinking for the last 48 hours. What if they use a contraption like a medieval guillotine? What if the two hooded men operating the guillotine are residency students with only a few hours of OR experience? What if the priest escorting me down the hall to the OR trips and sprains his ankle? These are times when I REALLY wish we had government-run health care. I'd be on a two-year waiting list right now.

Sincerely,
Chris

August 14, 2009

Dear Obama,

The vasectomy went fine. All my worry and anxiety was for naught. My recovery is going well so far, although I don't know if I'll ever look at a bag of frozen peas the same way again.

Sincerely,
Chris

DEAR OBAMA

August 21, 2009

Dear Obama,

I'm a little embarrassed by the lack of progress on my "Bald Awareness" campaign. I have a thousand excuses, but the only one with any merit is that I've started a new job. That being said, I'm proud to say that I finally devoted some time to write the following letter to send to my local congressman. Here's the first draft:

Name
Address
August 18, 2009

Dear Representative,

I am writing to urge you to support a proposal I've recently drawn up titled the "Follicle Stimulus Plan." This proposal is a comprehensive approach to combating the serious, yet neglected, effects of alopecia (aka baldness).

Not only is baldness devastating to the scalp, it can also destroy a man's soul. The emotional toll this silent beast has taken on those afflicted is incomprehensible. Yes, there are treatments, drug therapy options, and herbal remedies, but you tell me if copper peptides, ginkgo biloba, and the Chinese herb He Shou Wu is the best we can do.

President Obama's life story and election have given me hope that anything is possible, even a cure for baldness. I would not have said this during the last eight years, as I'm confident that the former president was an anti-baldite, among other things. I implore you to take a stand for the millions of people in this great country needlessly suffering from "eminent domain of the scalp." Please help make a statement and ask Washington to grant us our fundamental right to have hair.

Sincerely,
Me

Again, this is just a rough draft. However, when I do mail the final version, I'll include remnants of my own hair with a note that reads, "You think this is bad, imagine the source!"

Sincerely,
Chris

August 24, 2009

Dear Obama,

Wow! That is about all I can say regarding the successful conclusion to your "Cash for Clunkers" program. Despite the fact that 85% of the cars purchased under the program were foreign made, I still think this was exactly what the ailing American car industry needed. Although many dealerships are still waiting on the federal government to reimburse them the $500,000 – $1,000,000, it sounds like the car industry is back on track. At least we know it wasn't a handout.

DEAR OBAMA

Piggybacking on "Cash for Clunkers," I thought it might be productive to have the Feds run some sort of "Cash for Conservatives" program. You know, something to streamline the political landscape, silencing dissent as the ultimate goal. I don't know but I'm sure your henchmen could run with it.

How's Martha's Vineyard so far? I was pleased to see that you used some discernment only choosing a $35,000/week beachfront rental—not at all excessive and perfectly appropriate for these economic times.

I hope you brought your A-game. It looks like you will be hitting the links with a few colleagues and UBS CEO Robert Wolf. It's important that he puts aside the ongoing case against UBS, the one involving helping wealthy clients evade taxes for some golf. For some reason I wasn't at all surprised that he was and continues to be a major supporter of yours.

All I know is that you had better enjoy this vacation. You have a lot of stuff waiting for you back in D.C. Your first day back will most likely begin with questions regarding Attorney General Holder's appointment of a prosecutor to analyze a few cases in which the CIA may have violated anti-torture laws against a couple of terrorists after 9/11. This is in line with what you said back in April about the country moving beyond previous interrogation tactics. Holder has clearly stated that if there is any evidence suggesting that CIA operatives tormented detainees with images of Joy Behar, his Justice Department will prosecute the offenders to the fullest extent of the law.

DEAR OBAMA

About time . . .

Sincerely,
Chris

August 29, 2009

Dear Obama,

Al Franken is a United States Senator.

Sincerely,
Chris

September 7, 2009

Dear Obama,

Apologies are in order. My kids were not able to catch your address to the nation's schoolchildren two nights ago. However, we did work on creating and plotting several mural locations in your honor.

Apparently, teachers across the country were encouraged to ask their students several follow up questions to what you said. Basically, the kids were asked to write to you and ask how they can help with your agenda. Here are some of the more popular questions that teachers submitted:

DEAR OBAMA

- What is the President trying to tell you, and was Saul Alinsky really a genius?
- What would you like to tell the President, besides thanking him for "collective" salvation?
- What is the President asking you to do, and would you feel weird ratting out your parents if their political views differed from the President's?
- Is what the President is asking for reasonable, and how much do you think he can bench press?
- What are the great ideas from early 20th century European political ideology that the President challenges you to accept?

Although we did not watch your address live, we did DVR it. I submitted a few questions despite being a day late. I included one that may seem a bit odd when you see it, but I felt it was important: "Assuming the dimensions are regulation, would you be willing to play a game of shuffleboard on the face of Massachusetts Senator John Kerry?"

Sincerely,
Chris

September 9, 2009

Dear Obama,

Never have I seen such ignorance and bigotry in all my life. The way the media and opposition are treating your "Green

Czar" Van Jones is completely unacceptable, if not criminal. This is beyond partisan bickering. This is verbal aggravated assault. This honest, self-proclaimed communist has recently been singled out by hate-filled, knuckle-dragging neocons who cannot accept progressive ideology. For reasons unbeknownst to me, this truly patriotic American, who once referred to Republicans as "assholes" during a speech, is having his character and good name dragged through the mud.

As angry as all this nonsense makes me, part of me says, "Go ahead and waste your time trying to drudge up nothing." Am I'm supposed to be concerned that Mr. Jones said:

> I met all these young radical people of color, I mean really radical, communists and anarchists. And it was like, this is what I need to part of. I spent the next ten years of my life working with a lot of those people I met in jail, trying to be a revolutionary."

Oh, scary! Like I'm supposed to be offended when this proud 9/11 Truther said this about former president Bush:

> I hate to say this, and I hope I don't offend anybody, but the President of the United States sounded like a crackhead when he said that. I just... a little bit more ... just a little bit ... just a little bit more ... a little more ... a little more ... a little bit more petroleum. Like a crackhead trying to lick the crack pipe for a fix."

DEAR OBAMA

What's the big deal that he named his one-year-old son after African communist leader Amílcar Cabral, or that he was a supporter of convicted cop-killer Mumia Abu-Jamal, or that he described himself as a rowdy black nationalist?

I applaud the few members in Washington who backed this promising young man. One of your closest friends and longtime advisors Valerie Jarrett was the original talent scout that brought him on board. She was ecstatic when he arrived and said:

> We were so delighted to recruit him to the White House. We've been watching him really, he's not that old, for as long as he's been active out in Oakland and all of the ways and creative ideas that he has. And so now we have captured that and we have all of that energy and enthusiasm in the White House.

I feel horrible for Jarrett that her little protégé will not be around to introduce his "creative ideas" to the American people. I guess we'll all just have to sit around and wonder what could have been . . .

A lobotomy is the last thing David Gergen should consider after he said this about Jones' resignation, "It's a sad day to see a man of good work get so little credit." Not to be outdone, chemically balanced Howard Dean jumped in, claiming Van Jones was "brought down" and called his resignation a "loss for the country." I'm sure Dean was impressed when this little jewel from Jones was uncovered: "I'll work with anybody; I'll fight anybody if it will push our issues forward. I'm willing to forgo the cheap satisfaction of the radical pose for the deep satisfaction of radical ends."

What I really find comforting is the fact that Van Jones played a role in designing and executing the stimulus plan. I wonder if he incorporated his desired steps to move the country from racial integration to "reparations for slavery" to "redistribution of all wealth." Jeff Jones, the co-founder of the domestic terrorist group, the Weather Underground, also helped craft the plan through their Apollo Group (funded by George Soros). And yes, thankfully, Jeff Jones is also a self-avowed Communist.

Sincerely,
Chris

September 17, 2009

Dear Obama,

What a coincidence! What are the chances that you deny Eastern Europe the plans for a missile-defense shield on the same date (September 17th) that Russia invaded Poland seventy years ago during World War II? Since the Czech Republic and Poland are a few of our last reliable allies, this should bode well for future cooperation and partnerships. I'm sure the folks in these two countries (where these shields would have been built) are feeling much safer today.

I would like to affirm your alternative defense plan—using stimulus funds to send college students to camp in the forests between Russia and Eastern Europe. They've been instructed to text message the Pentagon at the first sign of a Russian attack. Obviously this is a much more effective and less offensive approach. These students will have the latest phone technology, a case of Red Bull, and a picture of a missile. In case their cover is compromised, they've all been armed with a pocket Rolodex of some of the most well respected law firms in the country. Poland and the Czech Republic may be initially hesitant about the strategy, but Code Pink has sent an envoy over to address any concerns or questions they may have.

Sincerely,
Chris

"In order to ensure citizens freedom of conscience, the church in the USSR is separated from the state. Separation of church and state. And the school from the church. So the church and the state are separate and the school from the church."

– Article 124 of the Soviet Union Constitution

September 22, 2009

Dear Obama,

Please tell me you have a plan for taking over the newspaper and magazine industries. Are you aware of the amount of garbage circulating out there? It is comforting to know that with your preferred political ideology there inevitably comes a government takeover of the publishing world. I know you're on the right track, but let's start putting the pedal to the metal.

I was heartened to see that Senator Ben Cardin of Maryland just introduced the "Newspaper Revitalization Act" (or the "Newspaper Bailout Act"). I must say this is a nice step towards seizing the industry. The proposal would allow newspaper companies to convert into nonprofit entities, which would ultimately receive large tax breaks and provide strictly leftist commentary. Of course this will have difficulty getting out of the Senate, but it's nothing Pelosi and the Gambino family can't handle.

If I seem a bit fired up over this, it's due to an article I recently read. The article was about America's so-called spiritual heritage. It argued that America's foundation is rooted in Judeo-Christian values. Clear-minded citizens know full well that a very small portion of our country's history was actually influenced by these values. You, Mr. President, I'm happy to say, have not given in to this blatant attempt at revisionist history. No past president has ever snubbed the National Day of Prayer, however many of us cheered when you did not participate. Those of us in the know, were delighted when you declared that we are not a Christian nation during a major speech broadcast around the world.

I have no doubt that your predecessors would be proud of the moral courage and honesty you've displayed thus far. In fact let's look at a few past quotes from Democratic and Republican presidents regarding our country's past:

- Andrew Jackson (D): "The Bible is the rock on which our Republic rests."

- Abraham Lincoln (R): "The Bible is the best gift God has given to men ... But for it, we could not know right from wrong."

- William McKinley (R): "Our faith teaches us that there is no safer reliance than upon the God of our fathers."

- Woodrow Wilson (D): "America was born to exemplify that devotion to the elements of righteousness which are derived from the revelations of Holy Scripture."

- Herbert Hoover (R): "American life is built, and can alone survive, upon ... the fundamental philosophy announced by the Savior nineteen centuries ago."

- Franklin D. Roosevelt (D): "If we will not prepare to give all that we have and all that we are to preserve Christian civilization in our land, we shall go to destruction."
- Harry S. Truman (D): "The fundamental basis of this nation's law was given to Moses on the Mount. The fundamental basis of our Bill of Rights comes from the teachings which we get from Exodus and St. Matthew, from Isaiah and St. Paul."

- Dwight D. Eisenhower (R): "Without God there could be no American form of government, nor an American way of Life."

- John F. Kennedy (D): "The rights of man come not from the generosity of the state but from the hand of God."

- **Barack Obama (D): "We do not consider ourselves a Christian nation."**

Let's hope, Mr. President, that you've started a long-lasting trend for future Oval Office occupants . . .

Sincerely,
Chris

September 23, 2009

Dear Obama,

Once again, we had another productive and memorable day at the UN. Nearly every great leader and human rights advocate gathered in downtown Manhattan to promote peaceful tyranny. All-Star peaceniks such as Mahmoud Ahmadinejad, Hugo Chavez, Fidel Castro, and Muammar Gaddafi were all in attendance as you graced the stage on America's behalf.

We were all unfazed as you again put America on the pedestal of mediocrity and apologies. Not only did your words touch those around the world, but they also brought heartfelt responses from the aforementioned fab four. Qadhafi, who addressed the assembly immediately after you, declared, "We'd be content and happy if Obama can stay president forever." Hear, hear! Fidel Castro lovingly stated, "He is a friend of mine." Good for you, Mr. President. My impression is that once you're in with these guys, you've got it made.

After your UN speech, I saw that college kids on the internet started a new drinking game. Apparently this is how it works: During your major speeches, participants are supposed to drink every time they hear you either apologize for the US or decry America's exceptionalism. Although it's become very popular, it's generally short-lived, as most players have passed out after the first fifteen minutes.

Coincidentally, there is a similar drinking game that hasn't quite taken off yet. It involves our esteemed former Vice- President, Al Gore. The rules of this game are a little more complicated, as they require visual verification. Ideally, while watching an Al Gore speech, players are supposed to drink any time they see a hint of pigmentation on Gore's face. Not surprising, all participants are home by nine o'clock, having driven home themselves.

Sincerely,
Chris

DEAR OBAMA

September 29, 2009

Dear Obama,

We had a very dramatic moment on Capitol Hill today. Florida Congressman Alan Grayson took the floor and told the truth regarding the GOP and health care: "The first part of the GOP's approach to health care is: Don't get sick. If you get sick, America, the Republican health care plan is this: Die quickly."

    Things got tense as Grayson concluded his address to Congress. Two burly men wearing all-white uniforms approached the podium. They handed Grayson a white robe and a pair of slippers and calmly told him, "It's time to go home now." At first he angrily resisted and began screaming "I am King George III and I desire what is good. Therefore, everyone who does not agree with me is a traitor." The two state employees escorted him out as peacefully as possible, but eyewitnesses said it wasn't pretty. While he was dragged away to a nearby van, he again screamed, "I can't go back! The crayons! There are too many crayons!"

Sincerely,
Chris

DEAR OBAMA

October 2, 2009

Dear Obama,

Where do I begin regarding your failed attempt to bring the 2016 Olympics to Chicago? On the bright side you made history once again. You were the first President ever to personally pitch a city to the Olympic Committee. On the other hand, you were the first and only President to ever lose such a bid. So I guess you made two historic records this past weekend.

I think you should be admired for going above and beyond for the good people of Chicago. The citizens of the Windy City should be proud that you have had only their best interest in mind. This has nothing to do about paying back your associates and cronies in Chicago who helped get you elected. I'm also certain you would have fought just as hard if the Olympics were to be held in Detroit, Dallas, or Houston.

It's hard to fathom that these committee members actually denied you and Michelle even as you tried to explain Obama exceptionalism. I think I speak for most of us when saying it's an utter outrage and reeks of Olympic racism. It is so obvious anyone can see this from a mile away. I trust that it will only take a day or two before your shakedown artists expose those responsible for this Obamanation.

Another unmistakable culprit is global warming. I'm hesitant to inject this into the debate, but you know as well as I do that odd weather patterns can cause poor judgment. It was only a matter of time before this environmental catastrophe would start affecting people's critical thinking. I mean, how in the world does one explain how right-wing hack Tom DeLay advanced past the first round in *Dancing with the Stars*?

It's getting bad out there, Mr. President. People are scared and they have good reason to be. You probably heard what the Mayor of Tokyo had to say the other day: "It could be that the 2016 games are the last Olympics in the history of mankind. Global warming is getting worse. We have to come up with measures without which Olympic Games could not last long." I guess it doesn't matter after all that you didn't get the bid. According to Mr. Ishihara, we probably won't be here anyway.

Don't think I forgot about W's role in all of this. Yes, there's racism and yes, there's global warming, but nothing can put the kibosh on one's Olympic bidding the way George W. can. I fear the IOC officials still associate this scoundrel with the US. You were in a no-win situation. In their minds, his mere presence on US soil is enough to disqualify us from hosting the 2016 games.

This rejection had nothing to do with you and Michelle bragging about Team Obama instead of Team America. The two of you promoted the US the best you could with quotes like, "Over the past few years the fundamental truth of the United States has been lost." Or with this one, "The USA is open to the world and to that end I have directed the full force of the White House and the State Department behind it. I want people to come away with the impression that America is an open and diverse society."

I know it stings a little, sir, but you gave it the old college try.

DEAR OBAMA

Now I'm just waiting for the headlines: "Blame it on B.O."

Sincerely,
Chris

October 6, 2009

Dear Obama,

You almost gave me a heart attack today. I had the TV on mute and saw you surrounded by people in white overcoats. I feared it was breaking news and that they were finally taking away Speaker Pelosi. I quickly turned up the volume to find out that they were just resident/medical students on a field trip from Havana. It was clever of you to give them white coats to wear before your big health care speech. Had the secret photographs of your aides handing them out not been leaked, we would have thought they were "real" doctors.

Sincerely,
Chris

October 9, 2009

Dear Obama,

Congratulations, Mr. Nobel Prize winner! That ought to shut up the right-wingers for a while. How can your critics not be impressed by this honor? Why are they complaining about the fact that you were nominated for this award twelve days after taking office? I could see if it had only been ten days or something, but we're talking nearly two weeks.

Clearly the non-partisan Nobel committee wasted no time in taking one last shot at former President George W. Bush. They were never big fans of his and rightfully blamed him for nearly all of the world's bloodshed. W. must be humbled knowing that during his eight years as President he never won this prestigious award. I can't help but picture the former Warmonger in Chief sitting in Crawford, Texas moping, knowing his name will never be listed alongside such past glorious winners as Charles Dawes, the man largely responsible for the rise of Nazism, Peacenik Yasser Arafat, "Weimar Jimmy" Carter, the leader of his own non-crime family Kofi Annan, and Al "I encourage robust debate on global warming" Gore.

I salute those above but with all due respect, they have not contributed to peace in this world like you have. Besides the havoc in Afghanistan, Iraq's jeopardized security (ever since you authorized the departure of a number of our forces), Iran's nuclear threat, North Korea's audacity to launch missiles, terrorists hell-bent on blowing us up, and Jon and Kate never further from reconciliation, this world has at no time been more peaceful.

Sincerely,
Chris

DEAR OBAMA

October 14, 2009

Dear Obama,

I'm not really one for games, but I think I came up with a fantastic idea for one. It's similar to the game, "Six Degrees of Kevin Bacon." In case you're not familiar with this, Wikipedia defines this as:

> A trivia game based on the concept of the small world phenomenon and rests on the assumption that any actor can be linked through his or her film roles to actor Kevin Bacon within six steps. The object is to make the connection as quickly as possible and in as few links as possible.

My game uses the same concept as Bacon's game, but instead of using the "Bacon Number" for the degrees of separation, I'm using the "Obama Number" (i.e. Obama's "shortest path" algorithm). And rather than link actors to Kevin Bacon, I link Marxist brethren to you. Here's my definition for "Six Degrees of Barack Obama":

> A trivia game based on the small world phenomenon and resting on the assumption that any Marxist figure can be linked through his or her advocacy of proletarian revolution to President Barack Obama within six steps.

What do you say we get started? We can begin with easy ones like your pastor Jeremiah Wright and Billy Ayers. Wright has preached Black Liberation Theology for years, and we know this ideology gets its foundational roots from Latin America, which focuses on the Marxist concept of perpetual class. We also know that Billy Ayers is a self-avowed Marxist and was quoted as saying, "I'm as much an anarchist as I am a Marxist." Actually, you get a twofer with Ayers, but we can talk about the anarchist separation game some other time.

How about Frank Marshall Davis, who once wrote to a friend, "I have recently joined the Communist party?" He was your first mentor and someone who gave you career advice. No problem. How about Mike Klonsky? Well he was an official blogger for your presidential campaign, and is not only a Marxist, but a Maoist as well. Again, we'll do the Mao game with Klonsky and your Communication Director/Mao sympathizer, Anita Dunn later.

All right, I think we're warmed up now. How about Dr. Quentin Young? If my records are correct he is your physician, friend, and a prominent member of the Communist/Marxist Bethune Club. What about Alice Palmer? Doggonit, she was your political mentor, and member of the Marxist front group, the US Peace Council.

This is not as fun as I thought it was going to be. Maybe we just have to delve into the past here. How about one of my heroes and underrated thinkers of his time Leon Trotsky? OK, now I know there has to be at least one degree of separation between you and Trotsky considering he died nearly seventy years ago.

Actually, let me get back to you. . .

DEAR OBAMA

Sincerely,
Chris

Note to self: Change title of game to "No Degrees of Separation from Barack Obama."

October 16, 2009

Dear Obama,

I did it! Check this out. You have no immediate personal connection to Leon Trotsky, although your friend, mentor, Trotskyite, and member of the Socialist Party USA, Leon Despres was an associate and friend of Trotsky. Did you see how I did that? It's one degree of separation! I knew if I had several hours and a research team I'd be able to prove there is one Marxist out there with at least one degree of separation from you. Yes, I'm excited about this discovery, but it may very well be an outlier. In which case, the title of the game shall remain, "No degrees of separation from Barack Obama."

Sincerely,
Chris

DEAR OBAMA

October 22, 2009

Dear Obama,

I've been on such a high lately given all of your plans for the country that my mind is on overload. I don't know if it's the euphoria affecting me, but I was wondering if there is any way for you to form a government within our existing government. I don't mean more bureaucracies within the government—which I'm pleased to see you're attempting—but more along the lines of a new governmental body to oversee the current government.

I know it sounds crazy, but think about it. Run it by your life coach Mr. Soros...

Sincerely,
Chris

October 31, 2009

Dear Obama,

Happy Halloween! I wish I had more time to write, but we're going to a costume party in a little bit. In case you're wondering, I decided to dress up as Leon Trotsky. I spent way too much time deliberating this, but I couldn't decide between Trotsky and Saul Alinsky.

Based on my admiration and past character acting of Marx, I'm sure you would have bet the ranch that I was going to go as Papa Bear himself. Yet I've been reading a lot about Trotsky, his friendship with Adolph Joffe, and the influence of *Pravda*. I actually feel sorry for the guy. He never really got the respect that he fully deserved. So this is my small way of honoring him. Plus it's an easy costume: grow out the goatee, put on a suit and a wig, throw on some Himmler specs and you're ready to go. Needless to say, I'm very excited and hope everyone enjoys my Veggie Schnitzel Wraps.

Sincerely,
Chris

P.S. We're back from the party and I can't sleep. The party wasn't as fun as I had hoped. First, no one could guess who I was. The closest guess was Weird Al Yankovic. I kept throwing out hints like the Bolsheviks, Aleksandra Sokolovskaya, The Treaty of Brest-Litovsk, but they just sat there with a blank stare—like most capitalist lemmings.

After a while, the host got a little suspicious and said, "Hey, I know what you're doing so get lost and take that Commie crap with you." I was initially thrown off guard, but managed to stand my ground. "You don't understand, Trotsky hated Communism. He was expelled from the Communist Party. Just take two minutes to read this pamphlet and you'll see what I'm talking about ... please!"

He still wouldn't have any part of it. We had no choice but to leave. We were only there for twenty minutes. I was certainly disappointed; however I did manage to stick a few "Proletariat Exploitation" pamphlets on the windshields of several of the guests' cars.

Since there is nothing to do and I'm bored, I have the

time to surf the net. I'm on the White House website and still can't find specific information. You really need to have a word with your IT department. For some reason the transparency downloads are still lost in cyberspace.

However, it is better than it used to be. Hillary recently shared (with our friends the Russians) the locations and access to many of our nuclear weapon sites. And of course, Vice President Biden did reveal the location of a secret bunker under the old US Naval Observatory. International transparency is thriving, it's just domestic transparency that remains a little behind schedule—except of course for the text messages between Vice President Biden and Former Secretary of State Madeline Albright.

Albright: did u respond 2 schumers halloween party evite?
Biden: not yet
Albright: what's the hold up?
Biden: i can't decide on a costume
Albright: i thought u settled on adam lambert?
Biden: i did, but jill didn't think it was appropriate
Albright: u have 2 make a decision soon
Biden: i know. i'll probably end up going as iron man
Albright: nice. i loved the movie
Biden: movie?
Albright: yes, the blockbuster w/downey jr.
Biden: ok? i'm going as the element iron. in support of anemia awareness.
Albright: wasn't that last year's costume?
Biden: that was 2 years ago. last year i went as sanjaya.
Albright: by the way, gore will be attending.

DEAR OBAMA

Biden: fantastic! i wasn't sure with his schedule.
Albright: yep. he'll b the 1 dressed as greenland's shrinking helheim glacier.
Biden: wow! i can't wait to c it.
Albright: i hear it weighs 115 pounds.
Biden: awesome. c u there maddie

Sincerely,
Chris

November 5, 2009

Dear Obama,

I'm going to hop on the Pelosi bandwagon and declare a victory in yesterday's off-year elections. Despite the thumping that democratic gubernatorial candidates took in Virginia and New Jersey, it was a glorious night. Not only did New Hampshire Coos County School District superstar mom, Beatrice Offenhoffer win PTA contributor of the year, but also Aaron Carter and Joanna Krupa advanced to the final four on *Dancing with the Stars*.

Speaker Pelosi has every right to be optimistic about last night's results. I'm certain she considers it to be a mandate on your current agenda. My opinion is that Corzine's loss in New Jersey is irrelevant. I know you spent all of last weekend campaigning for him in Jersey, but the fact that this dyed-in-the-wool liberal and incumbent Governor lost in the bluest of states just means you have too much star power. I think when voters got to the voting booth they were expecting to see your name on the ballot. When they didn't see Barack Obama as one of the options for New Jersey Governor they simply selected Chris Christie because his name is so easy to remember. They were probably disappointed later that night when they discovered that he was a Republican.

For the record, I have no doubt that you could be President of the United States, and simultaneously be governor for several states. First, we know you can multitask, look how you handled searching for both a White House dog and a new church at the same time. Second, you're a pragmatist, as most pundits concluded before and after your election. Any lingering ideas that you are a far left ideologue have long since been debunked.

Holding multiple governorships could be a hobby for you. I'm not saying govern all fifty states, but maybe a few of the really hip states like New York or California. Right now it seems that basketball is your only outlet, and honestly you are awesome. Nevertheless, it wouldn't hurt to be interested in some additional activities. I could be off on this assumption, but I have this funny feeling that you have an affinity for totalitarianism. You might want to give that a try.

I have to get going, but I couldn't let Democratic Congressman Jim Moran's recent comments go unnoticed. He was at a get-out-the-vote rally in Fairfax, Virginia a couple of days ago when he said, "I mean, if the Republicans were running in Afghanistan, they'd be running on the Taliban ticket as far as I can see." It's hard to believe that with supporters like Moran Creigh Deeds (D-VA) is down by twenty points in the polls.

DEAR OBAMA

Between Moran, CNN Host Rick Sanchez, and the break out performer of the year, Florida Congressman Alan Grayson, it will be a crowded field for the Political Darwin Awards this year. In any case, Olbermann finally has some stiff competition.

Sincerely,
Chris

"Ask not what your country can do for you, but what your country can do for everyone."

– Lefty Progressiveson

November 9, 2009

Dear Obama,

My wife and I just got back from celebrating our 10th wedding anniversary in San Diego. We were fortunate enough to stay at the historic Hotel Del Coronado. The hotel is over 100 years old and it has long been a destination for Hollywood, politicians, and dignitaries. If you haven't stayed there yet I highly recommend it. Besides, it might be good PR to have the people see you slum it for once.

If I had to pick a highlight from the trip I'd have to say it was hearing the news that Speaker Pelosi was able to strong-arm the House into passing the Healthcare Reform

DEAR OBAMA

Bill. It seems strange to have something political be the best part of an anniversary trip, but it just made everything perfect. I'm confidant my wife would feel the same way.

Imagine our surprise to hear that they held this vote at midnight on a Saturday night. Regardless of the timing, it just goes to show that when you put your mind to something with no bipartisan support, closed-door negotiations, 2,000 unread pages of red tape, and several large men named Vito, anything can be accomplished.

I know this process contradicts what you said back on the campaign trail about transparency, such as "no negotiating behind closed doors, but bringing all parties together and broadcasting those negotiations on C-SPAN." Yes, one could be a stickler and say you deceived the American people, but seriously, was anyone really going to watch C-SPAN?

Speaker Pelosi used just the right amount of totalitarianism in order to get things done in Washington. I hope other members of your administration were taking notes. Let the entire process be a lesson to those eager enough to make a difference.

Sincerely,
Chris

November 11, 2009

Dear Obama,

Just because you are the President of the United States,

why should you feel obligated to go to Germany for the twentieth anniversary of the fall of the Berlin Wall? I know you've been taking some heat for not going, but thank you for having the courage of your convictions. Besides, I bet we're on the same page, feeling lukewarm about the wall being torn down anyway.

Conversely, you have perfect attendance to all the sporting events and golf outings you've been invited to, as well as UN global meetings and functions. I suppose you could have squeezed a trip to Germany into your schedule if it was during Oktoberfest.

But without the beer, why bother? . . .

Sincerely,
Chris

November 18, 2009

Dear Obama,

I recently heard something so disgraceful that I thought for sure we were going to have our first re-education camp intern. Former UN Ambassador, John Bolton was on a cable news program and referred to you as, "the first post-American President." I don't know if he was purposely trying to stir up controversy, but his ignorance and scornful attitude was astounding. Everybody and their mother know that Jimmy Carter was the first "post-American President." I don't know what type of revisionist history this guy is trying to sell, but no one's buying it.

In "nothing to see here" news, Iran sentenced five people to death today for their part in the recent election disturbance. Shockingly, the good liberals and human rights advocates are nowhere to be found. If only the five Iranians were Gitmo detainees.

I'm hopeful the Tea Partiers will get a clue and learn something from Iran's crackdown. They need to know that there will be repercussions to their actions. You can't be at a public forum and raise your voice two to three decibels and not expect any consequences. If you're going to use Sharpies and assorted Crayola Crayons to make signs opposing government policies, then don't be surprised when you are labeled as Nazis and Tim McVeigh wannabes.

The Tea Party is all about hate speech. That's all it is. No matter how they try to spin it, it's all the same. Some of them even have the gall to bring their children to these disturbing rallies. Obviously, you have much more restraint than I do. If I were President, I'd be ordering the arrests of these parents for negligence and child abuse. These poor kids have no chance. They'll probably end up thinking that the First Amendment applies to everyone.

In more random news, give my best to Lael Brainard. I know she's been under a lot of stress since it has been discovered that she had some discrepancies with her tax returns. Hmm ... this makes five of your nominees who have had tax issues during the vetting process. She shouldn't be too worried however, because her situation pales by comparison to "Taxy Timmy." I don't believe her post as Undersecretary for International Affairs is in jeopardy after all, Geithner is still plugging along in charge of American policies on issues regarding the World Bank, the International Monetary Fund, and international tax treaties. It certainly pays to know low people in high places.

If nothing else, Mrs. Brainard must feel comforted knowing that she can attend the "tax-dodgers support group" with several other members of your administration. Speaking of your administration, isn't Brainard's husband, Kurt Campbell, a new member of your cartel? I heard he was confirmed a few months back as Assistant Secretary for East Asian Affairs. I wonder if they use the same tax guy?

Lastly, you obviously get an A+ for your first nine months as President. But don't think it's going to be a given every time. The new spending for your first nine months in office totals more than President Clinton's entire eight years. You know as well as I do that this could have easily been achieved in less than four or five months. I'll let it slide this time, but don't push it buddy.

Sincerely,
Chris

"What did the Grateful Dead fan say when they ran out of pot?"

"This music sucks."

– Unknown

DEAR OBAMA

November 25, 2009

Dear Obama,

It is nice to see Biden doing so well. Touring with Jimmy Buffet these past nine months has done him a world of good. Obviously the soothing smell and sound of Buffet's live concerts is just what the doctor ordered.

I understand that you are a big Grateful Dead fan. Why does this not surprise me? I imagine past Presidents diligently at work in the Oval Office while listening to classical and jazz. But I imagine you at your desk contemplating new and exciting confiscatory measures with The Dead and Jay-Z bumping and jamming in the background. I'm sure the work environment is still presidential, and only mildly reminiscent of your average frat house.

Sincerely,
Chris

December 3, 2009

Dear Obama,

Oh, Climategate. The rats on the right think they've found the silver bullet to debunk global warming. Supposedly, some hacker gathered hundreds of emails and data from the CRU (Climate Research Unit) and posted it all over the web. Apparently, the emails reveal how leading scientists and climatologists around the world have been hiding critical temperature data regarding global warming. Nice try guy, but you're a little late to the show. The "science" was "settled" a long time ago.

As details of the so-called fraud from University of East Anglia's CRU are discovered, detractors are flooding the internet with phony emails incriminating hard working researchers and "experts." In one email a prominent scientist admits to using a "statistical trick" to hide the decline in temperatures. Who cares? Al Franken used numerous "statistical tricks" to win his senate seat in Minnesota.

The Flat Earthers continue to produce additional evidence, with the mother of all emails revealed a few days ago. CRU head, Phil Jones wrote the following to fellow colleagues Michael Mann, Raymond Bradley, and Malcom Hughes in November of 1999: "I've just completed Mike's nature trick of adding in the real temps to each series for the last twenty years (i.e. from 1981 onwards) and from 1961 for Keith's to hide the decline."

Reassuring everyone, Jones immediately told *Investigative Magazine* that he had no idea what he might have meant a decade ago by the words "hide the decline." Despite the allegations, I see no reason for him to forego the millions of dollars he received for his "research."

Jon Stewart had a comical take on all of this. He said this the other night on the *Daily Show*, "Poor Al Gore—global warming debunked via the very Internet you invented."

My advice to you is to not even bother with this nonsense. Go to Copenhagen next week and push for the policies that administration members John "My Son Might Not Even See Snow" Holdren, Carol "We Want To Control Your Thermostat" Browner, and Steven "Let's Paint Roof Tops White To Absorb Heat" Chu have espoused for years.

Go get 'em sir ...

Sincerely,
Chris

P.S. In light of Mr. Chu's suggestion, I would not hesitate for a moment to paint my bald head white in an effort to curb global warming.

> *"We should seek by all means in our power to avoid war, by analyzing possible causes, by trying to remove them, by discussion in a spirit of collaboration and good will. I cannot believe that such a program would be rejected by the people of this country, even if it does mean the establishment of personal contact with the dictators."*
>
> *– Neville Chamberlain*

December 4, 2009

Dear Obama,

Fortunately, Tiger Wood's infidelity and the fact that it's not a real story, has kept "Climategate" off the media cycle.

DEAR OBAMA

We're now into the fourteenth day of the exposed "hoax" and the most we know about this "scandal" is that they lied, manipulated data, and received millions in funds. Sounds to me more like the groundwork for a political career.

I don't understand how people can be so obtuse when it comes to protecting the planet. Shouldn't they at least care about the children? Obviously they don't. If they did, they would be strong proponents of abortion (population control). For fewer kids equals a smaller carbon imprint. Will they ever get the point that one is to worship the earth and deny its creator?

Your Afghanistan speech was superb. Nothing shows strength and leadership during wartime than an exit timeline. This national address will surely make it into the archives of great wartime speeches. Your moment immediately catapulted you to the ranks of Churchill and Eisenhower. The parallels are uncanny, particularly to Winnie. In fact, unbeknownst to most historians, Churchill's famous speech during the blitz on London did not end with, "We will *never* surrender." There was a brief pause, and then he actually concluded with, "at least until spring holiday."

Sincerely,
Chris

DEAR OBAMA

December 9, 2009

Dear Obama,

Back in April I wrote an entry describing you as "The Oxymoron President." Today's entry is an amendment to that original one. The subject is our country's new "Safe School Czar" Kevin Jennings. You brought him in to your administration to help, well, keep our kids "safe."

Mr. Jennings founded and was Executive Director for GLSEN (Gay, Lesbian, and Straight Education Network). One of his many duties was providing a "recommended reading list" for school children. This included, but was not limited to, material on "bathroom sex between school age kids, preschoolers, and first-graders, promotion of promiscuity," and many other bits of sexual wisdom from the progressive spectrum. I have this nagging suspicion Jennings and the great pervert Alfred Kinsey would have gotten along great. I'm pretty sure Mr. Jennings is not a member of NAMBLA (North American Man/Boy Love Association); however, he has highly praised group member, Harry Hay.

This is all public knowledge, and yet he continues to help shape policy in public schools. Now you know I'm all about the Obama train, but this guy might be a little too progressive—at least for now. I'm not suggesting that you throw him out of your administration, but maybe you can send him on a special assignment. How about heading up a new GLSEN office in the heart of Saudi Arabia?

Sincerely,
Chris

DEAR OBAMA

December 14, 2009

Dear Obama,

Would you please thump Senate Majority Leader Harry Reid in the skull for me? Why in the world can't this guy garner the sixty votes needed to pass this current health care bill? Tell Harry he needs to go "Larry the Cable Guy" on 'em and "get 'er done." I am glad you invited all Senate Democrats to the White House tomorrow. My only advice for tomorrow's gathering is that you have Gillooly clearly visible to all those pesky moderate holdouts. They must be forced to understand the urgency of getting something, anything signed before Christmas—don't they know that we only have three more years before this panic-driven bill takes effect!

This whole debate makes me wonder if your top political advisor, David Axelrod and his family will continue to earn millions from drug lobbyists. I know your "Health Czar," Nancy DeParle, has only earned $6 million dollars over the last three years as a consultant for six major medical companies, including Boston Scientific, Medco Health Solutions, and CareMore Health Plan. Even Attorney General Eric Holder made a small fortune representing the maker of Oxycontin. You know, maybe I've been wrong all along about lobbying, cronyism, and corruption; there seems to be good money in it.

Lastly, with the good guys fighting to give uninsured citizens and non-citizens health care, why not go for government-run auto insurance next? The precedent will be set, and we all know there are plenty of uninsured motorists

DEAR OBAMA

out there.

Sincerely,
Chris

December 17, 2009

Dear Obama,

I'm getting conflicting signals Mr. President. As a supporter of yours, I'm down with the whole Marxist thing, but what's with the recent "Maoist Czar" and cabinet member picks? I guess my question is: Are you looking for Marxists or Maoists?

We know Mao is one of Communications Director, Anita Dunn's favorite "philosophers." We also now know that your "Manufacturing Czar," Ron Bloom agrees with comrade Mao about political power and how the free market is pure nonsense.

I have to be honest, Mr. President, I don't know if I can do the Mao thing too. I've got too much invested into this Marxism gig. I'll carry around "The Little Red Book," but I can't fully commit—not now—not with the kids in Little League and me starting my new job.

Sincerely,
Chris

DEAR OBAMA

"Trading political favors is part of the grease that makes government work."

– David Axelrod (Top Obama Advisor), 2005 op-ed

December 24, 2009

Dear Obama,

Congratulations on the healthcare vote today. It's unfortunate that it had to be done on Christmas Eve when the American people were too busy to pay attention, but props on the strategy. Like the politicians who voted today, I have yet to read the bill. I'm anxious to see if hair insurance made it into the final version. I know it's a long shot, but a man can dream, can't he? I see you're raising taxes on tanning bed companies ... that'll help.

I didn't think Harry had it in him, but he managed to find the sixty votes. I have to give credit where credit is due. It's a good thing that Senator Ben Nelson (D-NE) is not as greedy as Mary Landrieu (D-LA). Harry was able to buy Nelson's vote for a mere $100 million, one-third the amount it took to get Landrieu's support. Senator Chris Dodd (D-CT) was given $100 million for a hospital in Connecticut. Closing out this batch of health care vote giveaways, hospitals in Tennessee got $99 million as a payoff for Rep. Bart Gordon's (D-TN) vote.

The honesty, transparency, and moral integrity by which these sixty votes were garnered should silence those equating your administration with the mafia or your traditional crime family. Let's take a closer look at this. Wikipedia defines the Mafia as: "a loose association of criminal groups that share a common organizational structure or code of conduct."

When we break this down, "a loose association of criminal groups" could mean anything. It could mean a collection of unelected and unaccountable clan or "cosca" (Sicilian) of Czars. It could be a group of non-threatening offshoots of your administration such as ACORN and SEIU. It could also be a band of strong-arming lobbyists in D.C. (ironically enough, you have hundreds). The shared "common organizational structure or code of conduct" could also be anything. It could be the Gambino Family, the Genovese Family, the US Congress, etc. So as you can see, there are already plenty of question marks.

Lastly, your trump card against such ludicrous claims is your right hand man and Chief of Staff, Rahm Emanuel. Yes, we all know he sent a dead fish to a pollster who made him angry, but he has yet, as far as I know, to place the head of a dead horse in the bed of any media or political adversary (Note: This statement is only valid for actions that occurred on or before December 24, 2009, 3:47pm).

In closing, I must get a plug in for Florida Congressman Alan Grayson. He is making a valiant effort in his final push for the 2009 Political Darwin Award. In an effort to distance himself from the pack, he recently expressed desire for one of his critics, Angie Langley to go to prison. In a four-page letter sent to Attorney General Eric Holder, Grayson asked Mr. Holder to conduct an investigation. He asked that she be fined and imprisoned for five years. At this point, he knows he's won the award. He's just hot-

DEAR OBAMA

dogging it now.

Sincerely,
Chris

December 25, 2009

Dear Obama,

Merry Christmas ... I guess. Sorry to hear that you were not able to make it to church for Christmas Eve services. During this past year you've only attended church three times, and two of those times were to use the restroom. So why go for Christmas? I'm glad you didn't feel obligated to follow this silly little presidential tradition. As I've mentioned before, your indifference towards religious matters will hopefully start a new trend. Maybe next year, no one will feel obligated to go to church on Christmas Eve— leaving us more time for last minute shopping.

    You have told us that you have a strong Christian faith, so maybe it isn't indifference that keeps you from attending church, but rather that you haven't yet found a church you like. It's not that easy to find a place of worship led by a "spiritual leader" who spews anti-Semitism and damns the US. It's only been a year, so keep looking—there's got to be one out there somewhere. In any case, the significance of this holiday is waning and will soon be replaced by August 4th ... your birthday.

Sincerely,
Chris

DEAR OBAMA

December 28, 2009

Dear Obama,

America needs to count its blessings. As you know, a lone terrorist tried to blow up an airliner on its way from Amsterdam to Detroit. Apparently, he had a powder called PETN that is highly explosive and common among the "Freedom Fighter" community. Despite purchasing the ticket with cash, checking in without baggage, having his name on a watch list, and his own father contacting the US Embassy two months earlier to warn them about his son's extremism, he was able to pass all security points with no problem and board the plane.

Airport security was unaware that the powder was sewn to his underwear. Thankfully, an alert passenger jumped over a couple of people and subdued the potential suicide bomber before he could complete his mission. I'm not sure why this man, the other passengers, and the crew that foiled this attack are not paraded around as heroes. All I have seen are a couple of random interviews with a few passengers who described the situation as surreal and terrifying.

Rumors are now swirling that the "alleged" bomber has filed a lawsuit against the authorities that escorted him off the plane. His civil liberties lawyer was fuming as he addressed the media and described how his client's wrists still had small red marks from the handcuffs. He even exhibited a small box containing one of his client's arm hairs. He claims it was severed during the cuffing. Several legal experts say he actually has a pretty solid case and would not be surprised if the "victim" not only walked, but also was gainfully employed at any one of the Sbarros in downtown Manhattan.

As troubling as this story is, I sleep well knowing that casual outdoorswoman turned Homeland Security Director, Janet Napolitano is in charge. Her initial reaction was strong, clear and reassuring, "the system worked." This could have been a controversial statement, but as it turns out, she was only speaking on *Al Jazeera*.

Sincerely,
Chris

December 29, 2009

Dear Obama,

I would like to document Secretary of Homeland Security Janet Napolitano's clarification of her recent statement, referring to the failed terrorist attack, "the system worked". She has retracted her initial response and now believes the system did not work, and that her words were taken out of context. She also went on to say that her chartreuse turtleneck and dirty brown Members Only jacket were also taken out of context.

If only the above wardrobe combination was mere sarcasm. Sadly, it is not . . .

Good grief,
Chris

DEAR OBAMA

"Government is not reason; it is not eloquent; it is force. Like fire, it is a dangerous servant and a fearful master."

– George Washington

January 6, 2010

Dear Obama,

Why the country's flags are not at half-mast today I'll never know. One of the great statesmen of our times, Connecticut Senator Christopher Dodd, announced he is stepping down and will not seek reelection. In an emotional news conference, Dodd expressed gratitude for representing the good people of Connecticut for 35 years without ever seeing the inside of a prison cell. We all know by now that he was one of the key figures involved in the silly games at Fannie Mae and Freddie Mac. He was the top donor recipient the previous three years from these two institutions— John Kerry was number two, and you, Mr. President, were number three. . .you sly dog.

At the time, he was a top ranking member of the Banking Committee along with colleague Barney Frank. They both often expressed that Fannie and Freddie were "fundamentally sound financially." He expressed heartfelt sentiment about Fannie and Freddie in 2003, when he was said, "This is one of the great success stories of all time." Of course, he may have been referring to his two sweetheart-mortgage deals from Countrywide CEO Angelo Mizilo. I would never suggest that Senator Dodd had any involvement in the recent economic recession. I also find no humor or irony in the fact that in 2009 he outlined a plan for an independent consumer protection agency that would seek out and put an end to abusive financial practices.

We will all fondly look back on Dodd's distinguished career. Along with the aforementioned Banking Committee, he was a member of the conference committee that crafted the compromise bill that paved the way for AIG to pay out controversial bonuses. He initially denied his involvement, but the following day admitted he was a part of it. I believe his exact quote was, "Let me be clear—I was completely unaware of these AIG bonuses until I learned of them last week."

I guess if there is one low in Chris Dodd's political career it is that the Senate never censured him the way it did his father Thomas J. Dodd in 1967. Thomas Dodd is one of only six others who have been censured by the US Senate in the twentieth century. Although it was not much of a censure, because he had only converted campaign funds to his personal accounts and then spent the money. If I had extra time I would honor Dodd by acknowledging his father's lobbyist career for Guatemalan Dictator, Carlos Castillo Armas.

I am pleased knowing that in retirement Mr. Dodd will be able to spend significantly more time at his Irish cottage on the Island of Inishnee. In one of the great financial deals of all time, Mr. Dodd was able to purchase this ten-acre property for nearly 1/10 the going property value in Galway Bay. Mr. Dodd purchased the property through a business partner of Edward Downe, Jr. This fellow is a longtime friend of Senator Dodd's, and in the mid '80s they purchased a condominium together in D.C. A year before the Irish cottage purchase, Downe pleaded guilty to insider trading and securities fraud and agreed to pay the SEC $11 million in a civil settlement. Both were felonies. Senator Dodd successfully lobbied President Clinton for a full pardon for Mr. Downe. I have no reason for bringing this up, except that it is a nutty coincidence.

Sincerely,
Chris

January 7, 2010

Dear Obama,

I have a few more thoughts I would like to share concerning yesterday's entry. Pundits have suggesting that Senator Chris Dodd's retirement is indicative of forthcoming tough times for Democrats. I strongly disagree. We have a large pool of talented and exciting candidates who have the necessary prerequisites to replace honorable folks such as Chris Dodd. Here are a few examples.
    Let's take former Democratic Ohio Congressman and current felon, James Traficant. He was just released from a seven-year prison sentence for bribery, racketeering, and tax evasion. David "Diggler" Axelrod and Gillooly must be salivating over these credentials. It's not often you get a potential candidate who has the political trifecta of "must haves." In any case, I'm sure you were all thrilled to learn

that he would be running for Congress in 2010.

Democrats are calling current MSNBC host, Ed Schultz to run for Byron Dorgan's Senate seat in North Dakota. Democrats would love to bring him on board, considering he is all about civility and rationality. One of his claims to fame, aside from mastering the drinking game "Quarters," is last year's quote, "The Republicans lie. They want to see you dead! They'd rather make money off your dead corpse! They kind of like it when that woman has cancer and they don't have anything for her." How could you not go far in politics with logic like that?

I guess the point here, Mr. President, is I don't want you to worry about current Democrats jumping ship. As you can see, we have a strong bench that most pundits are underestimating. I mean for crying out loud, I haven't even touched on Rabbi Shmuley and his potential run for elected office.

Sincerely,
Chris

January 15, 2010

Dear Obama,

The family and I are flying to New England today. Our plane is currently in line waiting to takeoff. I wish my wife would do as they always did to B.A. Baracus and drug me before the flight. How wonderful it would be to eat a cheeseburger and a shake and finally wake up thousands of miles away.

Well, here we go. Engines are revving and we're headed down the runway. I still have no idea how these things take flight. I'm thankful for risk-takers and innovators who embrace the challenge to create. If civilization were a society of men like me, we'd still be marveling at the sight of fire.

We have a full flight, and with it a broad cross-section of society. I can't say that I'm all that impressed. I feel like we passengers better represent the bar scene from the original *Star Wars*. I don't know, maybe we're on some sort of transport to Mos Eisley? Anyway, it's at times like this that I really envy your access to Air Force One. It must be nice to know you can also utilize it for business purposes too.

Sincerely,
Chris

"[The GOP] are desperate to break this President. They have ardent supporters who are nearly hysterical at the very election of President Barack Obama. The birthers, the fanatics, the people running around in right-wing militia and Aryan support groups, it is unbearable to them that President Barack Obama should exist. That is one powerful reason. It is not the only one."

– Rhode Island Senator and 2009 Political Darwin Award nominee Sheldon Whitehouse

DEAR OBAMA

January 19, 2010

Dear Obama,

What a time to be in New England if you're into politics. This Scott Brown/Martha Coakley Senate race has been the talk of the town. I wish I could say the good guys won, but it looks like Brown is going to pull it off. This is the Massachusetts Senate seat vacated by the late Ted Kennedy. It's the seat he won reelection to nine times and held for 46 years. It's also the first time in 25 years that there's been an open Senate seat in Massachusetts. This was supposed to be a lock for Coakley, especially after you traveled to Beantown to campaign for her.

I thought for sure the last minute plea from Keith Olbermann was going to put Coakley over the top. Two nights before the election, he so eloquently laid out his case against Brown on *Countdown* with the following diatribe: "In short, in Scott Brown, we have an irresponsible, homophobic, racist, reactionary, ex-nude model, teabagging supporter of violence against women and against politicians with whom he disagrees." After receiving some flak from both the left and the right for this honest attempt at public discourse, Olbermann went on the air the next day and offered a sincere apology, "I'm sorry. I left out the word "sexist"—much to the delight of his dozens of viewers.

Now that I think about it, I had a dream about Olbermann last night. It was the weirdest thing. I dreamt that Keith was not real, but rather a myth, a figment of my imagination, similar to Keyser Söze. In my dream, fathers were using him as a spook story, or boogeyman to scare their children at night: "Rat on your pop and Keith Olbermann will get you."

Sincerely,
Chris

January 20, 2010

Dear Obama,

Congratulations! It's your one-year anniversary as President of the United States of America! Despite all the psycho haters out there, it's been a great year. Just the fact that Al Franken remains a United States Senator gives me hope for the State of our Union.

As for you and your amazing contributions to our country, where do I begin? In one year you've restored honor and integrity to the White House by holding such events as the "Beer Summit" on race relations, authorizing Tony Hawk to skateboard throughout the White House, allowing the Jonas Brothers to sleep in the Lincoln Bedroom, and permitting Ashton Kutcher to tweet from the White House. Oops, I almost forgot—your wife, Michelle Obama, became the only First Lady to ever appear on a reality show, *Iron Chef America* and the first to host a reality show at the White House, *Biggest Loser*. This is only a fraction of all the special events held at 1600 Pennsylvania Ave this past year. I never thought I'd see the return of *The Gong Show*, let alone it being produced from the White House. In any case, thank you Sir, I had forgotten how much I had enjoyed that program.

Your conviction and campaign promises are the only light in what seems to be a cynical view of politics. It's hard to find truth in Washington these days, let alone politicians who keep their promises. Who can forget when you emphatically told the American people on the campaign trail that lobbyists "won't find a job in my White House?" There certainly haven't been any, except for the dozen plus lobbyists currently working in your administration. But who's counting? You were also dead serious when you said, "Lobbyists no longer have a safe haven in Washington." Clearly you meant Washington State, because it was a banner year for lobbyists in general. K Street shattered last year's record, $3.3 billion, to lobby Congress and the federal government. This is very impressive considering the poor economy and that there are 1,500 fewer lobbyists around town. James Thurber, Director of American University's Center for Congressional and Presidential Studies, summed it up best, "It's the most active time that I have ever seen in the advocacy business." I can't wait to see what's in store for 2010!

You've also consistently broken records. Spending tops this list of unprecedented achievements, but other notable records will no doubt solidify your place in Cooperstown. How about the first bill you signed with a record breaking 9,000 earmarks, or the record total of executive orders you've handed down, or the record number of "Czars" you've personally appointed (even breaking Soviet and Eastern European records). However, the one record that truly captured America's heart was your appointment of the first transgendered person, Amanda Simpson, to an executive post. His/her new title is Senior Technical Advisor to the Department of Commerce.

America's ascension rolls on ...

Sincerely,
Chris

January 27, 2010

Dear Obama,

Splendid State of the Union address tonight! I've never seen such impassioned defiance from a sitting President before. One of the highlights for me was when you criticized the Supreme Court's recent decision on campaign finance. You said:

> Last week, the Supreme Court reversed a century of law to open the floodgates for special interests—including foreign corporations—to spend without limit in our elections ... Well I don't think American elections should be bankrolled by America's most powerful interests, or worse, by foreign entities. They should be decided by the American people, and that's why I'm urging Democrats and Republicans to pass a bill that helps to right this wrong.

DEAR OBAMA

The irony of your statement, of course, is that your campaign was actually paid for by special interests groups. You remember refusing to take any federal money, don't you? This allowed foreign corporations to donate to your campaign without limits. We saw them load your coffers to unmatched levels. So instead of the $80 million dollar cap, you were able to raise, what was it, $600 million? And only $200 million of that was undocumented—definitely not special interest or Soros money.

Let me get back to your public mocking of the Supreme Court Justices. The Right is furious over this and they have called this display a "breach of decorum." As invited guests of Congress, the judges had to endure being chastised for a court decision, something unprecedented for a President to do during a State of the Union address. Sorry judges, you should have known not to err on the side of the First Amendment.

I would love to analyze your entire speech, but I'm just not up for writing a dissertation tonight. In short, it was what I expected from a divine figure. You doubled down on your favorite projects: cap and trade, nationalized health care, and tax increases (aka spending freeze). You started anew with the American people by finally focusing on getting people back to work. After hearing that you invited Khloe Kardashian to the White House, I know you're as serious as a heart attack. By the way, what is it with you and Michelle and these reality shows? If I didn't know you any better, I'd think you were our Celebrity in Chief...

Sincerely,
Chris

DEAR OBAMA

"I propose a limitation be put on how many squares of toilet paper can be used in any one sitting. Now, I don't want to rob any law-abiding American of his or her God-given rights, but I think we are an industrious enough people that we can make it work with only one square per restroom visit, except, of course, on those pesky occasions where two to three could be required."

– Sheryl Crow, singer, environmentalist, global warming advocate

February 10, 2010

Dear Obama,

How about this weather! It seems the whole country is either buried in snow or getting hammered with torrential rains. The latter is hitting us right now. I'm born and raised in California and I've never seen so much rain in such a short amount of time.

I'm thankful we got out of New England when we did. Who knows how long it would have taken us to get home in all of this. What makes this weather so scary is the fact that global warming is intensifying these wicked storms. Take the headline I saw today: *"D.C. Snowstorm: How Global Warming Makes Blizzards Worse."* We live in very trying times. I don't know what it's going to take to wake people up to the truth. Seriously, how much snow has to fall before people realize the threat of global warming?

I know there are people out there trying to change the phrase "global warming" to "climate change." They're the same people promoting the "Jobs Bill" when in reality it's just another stimulus bill. It just proves how crucial propaganda is in hoodwinking the average folk. In fact, I've compiled a small list of terms that should help the masses better understand what's really going on:

- Climate Change = Global Warming
- Recovery Act = Stimulus Bill
- Spending Freeze = Tax Increases
- Jobs Bill = Stimulus Bill
- Simple Majority = Reconciliation
- Deficit Reduction Commission = Tax Hike

My favorite of course, is "climate change." It's definitely very crafty, but I fear if they succeed with the new term "climate change," it will take away from the core issue—that the earth is warming and we should be ashamed of ourselves. It just boggles the mind that the average citizen is simply not listening. There's certain arrogance behind this blatant disregard of "expert" advice. The "experts" have given us all the solutions we need to combat this "inconvenient truth:" using only one square of toilet paper, painting roof tops white, building giant space mirrors, minimizing divorces (MSU study—divorced households spend more in electricity), etc.

Sincerely,
Chris

P.S. Sorry to hear that the Global Warming Summit in D.C. titled, "Global Warming Impacts, Including Public Health, in the United States." was cancelled today due to snow.

God has a sick sense of humor I guess …

February 18, 2010

Dear Obama,

As if we needed additional evidence of how dumb the American people are CNN came out with a poll saying that only 6% of the American people believe that the stimulus worked. It's the one-year anniversary of this mega-successful economic aid package and the average person believes Sean Hannity over you. Aside from the high unemployment (17% real unemployment), trillions in debt, and Moody's talk about lowering the US's triple-A rating due to debt burdens, what can the average person point to? Even financial guru and all-around wizard, Vice President Biden has said the taxpayers "have gotten their money's worth." Case closed …

    Let me conclude this brief entry by quickly affirming the Democratic Party. Indiana Senator Evan Bayh has decided not to seek reelection. There are reports that the DNC is already recruiting superstar John Cougar Mellencamp to replace him.

Sincerely,
Chris

DEAR OBAMA

"The education of all children, from the moment that they can get along without a mother's care, shall be in state institutions at state expense."

– Karl Marx

February 21, 2010

Dear Obama,

I recently got into a dispute with a friend of mine about homeschooling. They've been doing it for the past couple of years and are very happy with the results. My arguments were a bit shaky, as I was not prepared with all of the data and studies from "experts" in the field. I promise that the next time I engage in such debate, I will be better informed. I'm kicking myself for not using the following quote from the Communist Party Education Workers Congress:

> We must create out of the younger generation a generation of Communists. We must turn children, who can be shaped like wax, into real, good Communists … We must remove the children from the crude influence of their families. We must take them over and, to speak fairly, nationalize them from the first days of their lives. They will be under the healthy influence of Communist Children's nurseries and schools. There they will grow up to be real Communists.

I believe Education Secretary Arne Duncan displayed this

quote on the outside of the DOE headquarters in Washington after he took over the department. He planned to have T-shirts made, but there were just too many words, plus most in the department have trouble reading anyway.

Nevertheless, spending the evening arguing with my friend was unpleasant to say the least. I tried to explain to him that they weren't giving their children much of a chance if they, as the parents, were teaching them morals, character, and love of country. For it is obvious that this should all be left to the state. As flustered as I was, I did manage to remember a couple of irrefutably wise quotes such as: "Education is a weapon, whose effect depends on who holds it in his hands and at whom it is aimed." (Vladimir Lenin) and "Give me four years to teach the children and the seed I have sown will never be uprooted." (Joseph Stalin).

Sincerely,
Chris

"During that period [1930s] of Nazism and fascism— a real danger to the United States and democratic countries around the world—there were people in this country and in the British parliament who said, 'Don't worry! Hitler's not real! It'll disappear!'"

– Self-proclaimed Socialist Senator Bernie Sanders on global warming deniers

DEAR OBAMA

February 24, 2010

Dear Obama,

Do you know why America loves Vice President Biden? It's because he represents the average American, a "blue collar special," if you will. That's what endeared people to him during the campaign. Give him a hard hat, a shovel, and a plan and he's good to go. So I wasn't surprised at all to hear about his off the cuff remark today during your much-anticipated Health Care Summit. I guess in an unscripted moment Vice President Biden was overheard telling someone, "It's easy being Vice President— you don't have to do anything." I'm just thankful Palin never got near the White House.

In my humble opinion, your summit was a huge hit. In a bipartisan effort, you managed to gather both leading Democrats and Republicans to discuss health care reform. In the footage I saw, it all seemed quite constructive. Thoughts and ideas were volleyed back and forth, with only the occasional interruption by Vice President Biden announcing, "And this ... is American Idol!"

If we could only get the American people on board this would be a done deal. I'm impressed you and other members of Congress are defying public opinion. Reconciliation, or the "nuclear option," has to be done— I'm sorry but the ends justify the means. Although you work for us, it's clear we the people need a little more time to realize that health care reform is what's best for the country (and for your power grab).

I remember back in May of 2005 (during the

Republican majority) Vice President Biden saying, "This nuclear option is ultimately an example of the arrogance of power. It is a fundamental power grab." He also said, "I say to my friends on the Republican side you may own the field right now but you won't own it forever. I pray to God when the Democrats take back control we don't make the kind of naked power grab you are doing." I think we can all agree that his prayer has been answered.

Stay strong Mr. President. Don't let the ignorant masses get to you. It's only polling. Besides, Soros and Rahm should have that new Vote-Circumventing device up and running in no time. Ironically, it seems like only yesterday when you, the Democrats, and the Left in general were shouting that the American people wanted out of Iraq. You referenced polls and accused W. of being a fascist and ignoring the will of the people. Yes, the parallels are there, but these are completely different circumstances—the will of the people doesn't matter right now—because when it comes to health care reform, you're right, and the people are wrong.

Sincerely,
Chris

March 5, 2010

Dear Obama,

Once again health care reform takes center stage. And why shouldn't it? If it all works out like you hope, health care

DEAR OBAMA

reform should be here by April. In which case, you will have only spent 1/3 of your entire presidency working to change our entire health care system, something the people overwhelmingly don't want—well they do—they just don't know it yet.

What I find most clever about your health care plan is how it won't take effect for three years, but we'll start paying taxes on it now. I find this brilliant because you can use the next three years to apply this money towards "debt reduction" without any real plans to cut spending. That should get your detractors off your back regarding fiscal responsibility.

Along with this never-ending health care debate, we also had an upbeat unemployment report in which "only" 36,000 people lost their jobs in January. Senate Majority Leader Harry Reid was so impressed he went on national TV and said the following, "Today is a big day in America. Only 36,000 people lost their jobs today, which is really good." (On his way back to Weaseldom, Reid congratulated a man who "only" needed a triple-bypass)

What was it you recently said about focusing like a laser beam on jobs? It's a bummer that instead you end up having to focus on health care and other pressing issues, like your upcoming movie night with Steven Spielberg and Tom Hanks.

Sincerely,
Chris

DEAR OBAMA

March 7, 2011

Dear Obama,

I would like to offer my best wishes to America after hearing that you brought SEIU union leader, Andy Stern into your administration. I believe it's only fair, since his union funneled, what, $60 million to your election campaign in 2008? Stern is now a member of the prestigious "National Commission on Fiscal Responsibility and Reform" which will analyze and recommend ways to whittle down the federal government's $12 trillion debt. The first commission was disbanded for suggesting that Washington not get into debt in the first place.

Interestingly enough, there is a small controversy brewing over Stern's appointment because of his lobbyist ties—well, make-believe ties. He's only dealt with government officials through public records, White House logs, Twitter messages, press reports, and union report disclosures filed with the Labor Department. Investigators found that he spends more than 20% of his time contacting policy makers and elected officials. Some critics cite the fact that Mr. Stern has visited the White House 22 times this past year. The 2008 Federal Lobbying Law states that one must register as a lobbyist if they spend this much time trying to influence government. Failure to register as a lobbyist could result in up to five years in prison, and/or a $200,000 fine—or a position in your administration.

Knowing that Andy Stern and George Soros are members of the White House Frequent Visitor Program, one can be

DEAR OBAMA

certain that America's best days are ahead . . .

Sincerely,
Chris

March 11, 2010

Dear Obama,

Would you please get rid of this Eric Massa character? His bogus allegations against his own party (Democrats), and more specifically Rahm Emanuel, of intimidation are shaky at best. Whether he is telling the truth or lying, he should know better than to go against the family. If you ask me, this guy got off pretty lucky considering his confrontation with Rahm in the congressional showers. He very easily could have received a Rahmbo special. All I have to say to this ex-Congressman is, "Keep your mouth shut, the Obama Nostra is out there."

I see you're considering another executive order to regulate recreational fishing. It's been so long since yesterday's executive order that I thought you had forgotten about them. Today's executive order, brought to you by the makers of Iron and Curtains, will prohibit US citizens from fishing in the nation's oceans, coastal areas, Great Lakes, and some inland waters. However, the Interagency Ocean Policy Task Force has yet to issue its final report on *zoning* uses of these waters.

I like this strategy much better. Instead of immediately going after rednecks with guns, let's go after rednecks with fishing poles. Since terrorists are plotting to kill us, unemployment is through the roof, our economy is on life-support, there is an impending new health care system, now is the perfect time to address this ticking time bomb.

It's clear our mainstream environmentalist friends—folks who refer to fish as "sea kittens" and ride around on arugula-powered Vespas—have influenced you. I'm pleased to see that you're finally listening and seeking wise counsel from moderate pragmatists who value wheat germ as much as they do mankind. Now that you're on course to regulate fishing, dust and hedge clippings might be the only remaining things in need of suffocating regulations. Your success in regulating banks, Wall Street, compensation, the auto industry, soap, air, and now water, has finally given me hope that there is a light at the end of this capitalistic nightmare.

Sincerely,
Chris

March 13, 2010

Dear Obama,

Speaker Pelosi has been busy this past week. She's pretty much used all her political capital on health "insurance" reform. She is definitely putting all of her Botox in one basket, or all her eggs in one eyelid, or … you know what I mean. I'd like to share with you three of her latest memorable quotes:

- "We can have bipartisanship without bipartisan votes."
- "We need to pass this [health care] bill so we can see what's in it."
- "We Democrats share some of the views of the Tea Party movement."

The last quote was particularly confusing considering she's referred to the movement as "Astroturf" and Tea Party members as Tim McVeigh wannabes and Nazis with swastikas in hand. In her defense, CVS/pharmacy has had several back orders lately.

Don't get me wrong, I agree with her. In fact, I wish she would take her fight to CBS or NBC and pitch a new reality series titled, *The Real Tea Partiers of America*. I feel the American people need to know who and what is really behind this dangerous movement. It's the same concept as other reality shows. Camera crews could follow stay-at-home moms running errands to Costco, the dry cleaners, and picking up the kids from school—documenting their mischief every step of the way. They could venture over to the local senior center to catch up with some of the older more experienced riffraff as they play bingo, drink Ensure, and take naps, all the while plotting their disruptive outbursts for the next town hall meeting. And last but certainly not least, homeschoolers. Whichever network picked up the pilot would be wise to preface the footage with a warning: "Graphic material. Involves unedited footage of kids actually learning math, English, science, writing, economics, and non-revisionist history. May be unsuitable for viewers in Marin County."

DEAR OBAMA

The success of the Tea Party has given me hope for something I've been mulling for some time. I think the timing is right to launch the BEA Party movement. The Bald Enough Already Party is probably my last hope.

More information to follow...

Sincerely,
Chris

March 18, 2010

Dear Obama,

I've had a strange morning. While listening to Falco's, "Rock me Amadeus" during my drive to work, one thing finally made sense to me: Republicans hate black people. I've never really given it much thought until this health care debate. It's clearly been the theme of the talk shows I've been listening to lately. The reason you cannot get any bipartisan support is not because of your political agenda, it's because of the color of your skin.

I would actually take it a step further and say that their hatred for Speaker Pelosi tells me they're racist towards all over-medicated, middle-aged, yentas from the Bay Area. Their disgust for Jimmy Carter suggests that they're racism also includes peanut-farming pacifists. Who knows, maybe they have their cross hairs set on all legume farmers?

For those who have had their head stuck in the sand the past five to ten years, let me make it clear that Bush is responsible for this resurgence of racism. Ask any liberal and I guarantee 80% of them will tell you that Former President George W. Bush hates African-Americans. How could they think otherwise? After all, he only nominated the first black Secretary of State, Colin Powell, and the first female black Secretary of State, Condoleeza Rice. As any liberal talk show host will tell you, these two are not real African-Americans, but the fake conservative kind.

More evidence of W's indignation towards the black community was his commitment to Africa. He had the gall to champion the PEPFAR (President's Emergency Plan For AIDS Relief) program in which he committed $15 billion, resources, and programs in the fight against HIV/AIDS. Conservative estimates say that a meager three-to-five million African lives have been saved by his efforts. Continuing on, the former President's Millennium Challenge Corp. identified nine African countries to receive roughly $4 billion towards infrastructure and agriculture. Additionally, he went on to implement the African Education Initiative that trained nearly one million teachers, gave hundreds of thousands of scholarships for girls' education, and provided more than ten million textbooks. Finally, W's reign of terror in Africa concluded with his Malaria Initiative, which reportedly only saved hundreds of thousands of lives in the countries of Tanzania, Uganda, and Angola.

With such an obvious disdain for the people of Africa, and black people in general, it's not surprising that he only garners an 80% approval rating there. Sadly, the streets they named after President Bush in certain African cities will forever be sobering reminders of the racist American cowboy who left behind a catastrophic path of survival, hope, and gratitude.

Sincerely,
Chris

"In my many years I have come to a conclusion that one useless man is a shame, two is a law firm, and three or more is a Congress."

– John Adams

March 22, 2010

Dear Obama,

219 – 212, the Health Care Bill passes! Words can't even explain how I feel. It's the same feeling one gets after downing a bottle of Worcestershire Sauce in eighteen seconds—not that I've ever tried.

Let this victory be a lesson to all those greedy insurance companies and any other blood-sucking corporations brazen enough to take advantage of the system. I don't know how they thought they were going to continue to get away with earning an average profit of 3% last year. They had it coming to them if they believed that the people were just going to stay quiet and watch "Capitalism Gone Wild."

And may I say, what a tribute to the late Ted Kennedy. Health care reform was his mission in life, so he would be incredibly proud of you. It is ironic that Kennedy was the one who invented HMOs back in 1973 and had his fellow Democrats' support. I have to believe that at the time he had no idea that a 2% plus in profits was possible with such a system. In his defense, he clearly would never had proposed such an idea if he had known the potential profit windfall.

This is just awesome. Everybody is talking about your health care victory, and rightfully so, but there is another important success with this win: you've managed to demonize the word "profit." Perhaps most important is that this Health Care Bill highlights some of the Marxist utopian ideals I have grown to love such as collectivism and redistribution of wealth. Oh, almost forgot, it also permits sex offenders to get Viagra. What a bill!

As a bonus, with this one vote you've regained any political capital you may have lost along the way. To achieve what you did—winning by seven votes—while having large majorities in the House and Senate speaks volumes. Of course, as much as you deserve praise for this win, there is one other individual who was just as instrumental. Please offer my sincere congratulations to Speaker Pelosi for all of her hard work, and for ultimately coming through for the American people. Aside from Lex Luthor, I can't think of any other American who has done more for the people.

Some are criticizing you both saying that there was no bipartisanship in this bill. This actually couldn't be further from the truth. There was absolute bipartisanship—35 Democrats joined all 177 Republicans in opposition. You should both be proud that for the first time in modern history a major bill has passed without one single Republican vote. Even LBJ was able to get nearly half of the Republicans to sign on to Medicare in 1965.

It's a shame that anyone would be focusing on this, while ignoring the fact that all the different factions of the Democrat Party—the Maoderates, Red Dogs, and Regressives—ultimately came together for the good of the nation.

Sincerely,
Chris

March 26, 2010

Dear Obama,

Have you heard the good news? We (California) are most likely going to vote on the legalization of marijuana in November. There's nothing that our state needs more than additional potheads running around. We can certainly use more in the universities, legal profession, Hollywood, etc. The timing is good too, because as the 2012 election rolls around, I feel pretty confident that the weed vote is yours to lose.

I almost forgot to mention the deal you made with the trustworthy Russians today. In your ceaseless effort to show off America's strength to the world, you announced a new treaty with Russia, which will replace the Strategic Arms Reduction Treaty (START). This will be the largest nuclear disarmament the US has had in decades. Basically the US will reduce its nuclear weapons by 1/3, while China, Iran, and North Korea continue to increase and strengthen their military and weapons arsenals.

By the way, what did you think of Fidel Castro's endorsement today? I heard he said that the bill was a "miracle" and wondered why it took America 234 years to pass it. He also said that its passage represented a major "success" for you. I couldn't agree more.

A good day all around, Mr. President . . .

Sincerely,
Chris

April 1, 2010

Dear Obama,

I see one of the Health Care Reform "yes" votes, Congressman Hank Johnson (D-GA), is looking to participate in this year's Political Darwin Awards. During a House Armed Services Committee hearing, Johnson was addressing Admiral Robert Willard, commander of the Navy's Pacific Fleet, when he expressed his concern about the island of Guam: "My fear is that the whole island will become so overly populated that it will tip over and capsize."

Congressman Johnson has visited Guam and was stating his concern that the influx of military personnel would overwhelm the island's infrastructure and ecosystem. His office has since said that Congressman Johnson was only joking. However they did not clarify if he was joking about the comment, or about being a member of Congress. The media have conveniently left out the fact that Congressman Johnson is part of the DHARMA Initiative (*Lost*). Although capsizing is a definite concern, it's nothing compared to the threat the "others" pose to the island.

We know if Johnson was a Republican and said something like this, the media would surely give him the same benefit of the doubt. Besides, it's well known around Washington that Congressman Johnson is the W.C. Fields of Congress.

Happy April Fools' Day—especially to the people of Georgia.

Sincerely,
Chris

"Iran, Cuba, Venezuela? These countries are tiny compared to the Soviet Union. They don't pose a serious threat to us the way the Soviet Union posed a threat to us."

– President Obama, May 18, 2008

DEAR OBAMA

April 7, 2010

Dear Obama,

Carpal tunnel is a foregone conclusion at this point. I had no idea you would produce this much material on a daily basis. Today's topic—nuclear deterrents. A couple of days ago you proved once again to the world that you are indeed the Commander in Chief, and not just some far leftist ideologue. You announced a new US policy: nuclear retaliation is off the table in the event of a biological, chemical, or crippling cyber-attack.

Predictably, the Right is denouncing your decision. The right-wing talking heads are in a frenzy arguing that this puts us all at risk and gives terrorists a green light to attack. Rubbish. As far I can tell, you kept in place our biggest deterrent, strategically placed holograms of Henry Waxman. Certainly the holograms, conciliatory language, and a stockpile of sparklers and Whistling Petes, will thwart any outside threat.

When will your critics understand that you are a modern day Sun Tzu—except that you actually know what you're talking about? I think it's safe to say you're rewriting the *Art of War* each and every day. In fact, your decision proves the fallacy in Tzu's writings. He said, "It is through the dispositions of an army that its condition may be discovered. Conceal your dispositions, and your condition will remain secret, which leads
to victory; show your dispositions, and your condition will become patent, which leads to defeat." Sounds like a little too much Tsingtao, Mr. Tzu.

DEAR OBAMA

It would be interesting to get his assessment on how you're doing thus far, at least from a strategic point of view. Not that he or any military mind could find fault with you alienating our biggest ally Israel (not to mention Bibi himself), taking the side of the communists in Honduras, refusing to endorse England's sovereignty over the Falkland Islands (thus taking sides with Hugo Chavez, et al.), giving Poland and the Czech Republic the bird in regards to a missile defense system, being completely transparent when it comes to our national security secrets, cutting our biggest arsenal deterrents, etc.

I see a third best seller, Mr. President: *The Art of Appeasement...*

Sincerely,
Chris

April 15, 2010

Dear Obama,

The much anticipated Nuclear Security Summit has just ended, and with it, a new hope for the world! Officials from forty-seven nations, and many other top envoys gathered in Washington this week to tackle the nuclear weapons situation. Each day the media raised our expectations with quotes such as, "An enormously productive day," or "A day of great progress." After much fanfare, the "historic" summit concluded with this statement, "We reaffirmed that it is the fundamental responsibility of nations, consistent with their international obligations, to maintain effective security of the nuclear materials and facilities under our control." I heard you also managed to get all 47 nations to agree that the cheetah is the fastest land animal—impressive indeed!

It reminds me of the success you had in Copenhagen with the "historic" global warming summit. Again, nothing of substance was achieved; however, attendees did receive a cool recycled arctic brush tote bag.

Anyone still uneasy about the worldwide nuclear arms race clearly did not hear you say: "We have seized this opportunity, and because of the steps we've taken—as individual nations and as an international community—the American people will be safer and the world will be more secure." As awesome as you were and as much as you tried, there was still no breakthrough with Russia and China concerning tougher sanctions for Iran, or regarding North Korea's unabated nuclear ambitions. But that doesn't matter because, Mr. President, we are relieved that you were able to convince rogue nations such as Canada, Chile, and the Ukraine to dump their nuclear stockpiles.

I just wonder if England and Israel (our two biggest allies) and Iran and North Korea (two biggest foes)—or is it the other way around— felt left out. It seems to me had these four nations also been present, the negotiations would have truly been historic.

One thing I've noticed recently is that just about everything you do is considered "historic." Conferences such as the National Security Summit, Copenhagen, and the Beer Summit obviously come to mind. Yet here are a few headlines you may have missed: "President Obama Shoots Historic Jump Shots at Local Georgetown Gym," or "President Obama Eats Historic Salami and Cheese Panini on Fourth Avenue" and "Cameras Catch Obama Taking a Historic Nap on Air Force One."

Sincerely,
Chris

April 20, 2010

Dear Obama,

Happy National Weed Day! I was never aware of such a day, but apparently it's been around since 1971. "420," as it's called if you're cool, was oddly enough started by some teenagers in the Bay Area. The day has evolved into a counterculture "holiday" when people gather to celebrate and smoke pot. The celebration is worldwide with the University of Colorado in Boulder leading the way. Other popular spots are Ottawa and Ontario Canada, where activists gather on Parliament Hill and smoke, consume, and snort cannabis. What I find shocking is that MSNBC is the only network reporting this news. Then again, every day at MSNBC is National Weed Day.

On another note, I had my annual doctor's appointment today. I was worried that my blood pressure would be high, but thankfully it was nearly perfect. I was surprised because I suffer from white coat syndrome. It never fails; every time I walk through those doors I start getting a little anxious. One might also say I'm a hypochondriac, but I wouldn't go that far. I just tend to excessively worry about having a serious illness.

My doctor didn't waste much time before he began railing on the health care bill. As I listened to his diatribe I couldn't help but think to myself, what do you know about the medical industry? How could you think that you or the rest of the medical community know more than the President and every other non-medical contributor to this bill?

He rambled off example after example of how this bill is going to affect his practice. I would have defended you sir, but I was hooked up to an EKG. That graph would have looked like the San Andreas "Big One" had I engaged him. It was a challenge, to say the least, but I kept my composure. It's not worth debating it anymore, especially since it's a done deal. It's time to move on to more important issues, such as the financial reform bill.

I'm glad to see Chris Dodd has taken the lead on this one. Who better to draft a financial reform bill than one who has already proven his brilliant ability to tinker with economic issues (housing crisis)? As much as he deserves credit for this bill, your fingerprints are all over it too. If passed, the government will have unprecedented power to control the private sector, which will include complete authority over the banking system.

Not surprisingly, you're already facing fierce resistance. It wasn't looking good until just a couple days ago, when out of nowhere the SEC announced charges against Goldman Sachs for fraud related to the subprime mortgage securities fallout. Wow, what a coincidence. The timing could not have been better. We needed some fresh, negative publicity to rile up the folks. Who wouldn't want to support a bill that goes after these big bad greedy corporations?

You must have mixed emotions about the charges against Goldman, considering it was the largest contributor to your presidential campaign. What was it, nearly a million dollars? Not bad, that's only seven times the amount W. received from Enron. Speak of the devil; I see you've already played more rounds of golf (32 rounds in sixteen months), than President Bush did during his entire eight years (24 rounds).

Keep "burning that midnight oil," sir. . .

Sincerely,
Chris

> *"America is a whorehouse ... where the revolutionary ideals of your forefathers ... are corrupted and sold in alleys by vendors of capitalism."*
>
> *– Red Dawn (as seen on Congressman Henry Waxman's bumper sticker)*

DEAR OBAMA

April 28, 2010

Dear Obama,

No one can ever say you're not a student of history, Mr. President. With financial regulation close at hand, you addressed Wall Street stating, "Now what we're doing—I want to be clear, we're not trying to push financial reform because we begrudge success that's fairly earned. I mean, I do think at a certain point you've made enough money." No doubt, that is straight out of the Founders' writings.

 Speaking of Wall St., I wish more citizens could have watched as Michigan Senator Carl Levin took center stage at the Goldman Sachs hearings. He headlined this Soviet style show trial. His swearing, mockery, and fake outrage was reminiscent
of something you would see on the History Channel.

 Bravo for sneaking former White House Counsel, Greg Craig over to Goldman Sachs. I can't believe the media let that
one go under the radar. It's a good thing because people might have remembered you saying on January 21, 2009: "When you leave government, you will not be able to lobby my administration for as long as I am president." It's reassuring to know that all communication with Mr. Craig will cease.

 Actually, when you really look at it, it's quite ironic how many connections there are between Goldman Sachs and the White House. Goldman partner Gary Gensler is head of the Commodity Futures Trading Commission. Former Goldman lobbyist, Mark Patterson, is Timmy

DEAR OBAMA

Geithner's Chief of Staff at the Treasury. Former co-chairman of Goldman Sachs, Robert Rubin, is a permanent White House fixture and is constantly giving Geithner advice. Even Gillooly has ties to Goldman; the financial giant kept him on a monthly retainer when he worked as Clinton's chief fundraiser. No wonder Goldman has been your top donor all of these years.

Sincerely,
Chris

P.S. By the way, congratulations to you for getting the financial regulation bill passed. This Keynesian piece of legislation would make Old Maynard proud.

May 1, 2010

Dear Obama,

Happy May Day! What's May Day some may ask? Well, for anyone who's been living under a capitalist regime the past fifty years, May Day, or International Workers Day, is a day when trade unions, labor activists, communists, socialists groups, and anarchists promote increased awareness in the industrial workplace. It's an international celebration of the social and economic achievements of the labor movement. In other words, "The Obama Doctrine." In 1958, Congress made Loyalty Day an official holiday. Fifty years later, protest and unrest round out the celebration. Like National Weed Day, Boulder, Colorado is the best place in the US to observe this holiest of anti-capitalist days.

There is one group that believes May Day is too narrow in its scope. This environmental/ anti-greenback group got off to a slow beginning. Initially they referred to themselves as the Green/Anti-green Movement. It wasn't until they officially changed the name of the group to the Green/Anti-darker Green Movement that the public started taking them seriously.

Early on critics labeled them as elitists who were racist towards traditional forms of exchange. Organizers and promoters were appalled at the accusations and cited the movement's mission statement of "a world without monetary classes equals a fairer and more barter-friendly world." Detractors were primarily against G/ADGM's goal of having the country on the "chicken standard" within ten years. Naturally, PETA put up a vigorous court battle; the two sides ultimately settled out of court. It agreed to drop the "chicken standard" and any other poultry standards, in exchange for PETA's financial and logistical support in an effort to push the country towards the "incense standard."

In any case, the group is currently flourishing and recently held its 7th annual Currency Sux Day. Every May 1st followers of the Green/Anti-darker Green Movement gather outside the US Mints throughout the country, and from 10:00a.m. until 10:01 a.m. proceed to tear up all denominations of US currency. Ironically, afterward the group is forced to panhandle for lunch money and bus fare.

Sincerely,
Chris

DEAR OBAMA

May 2, 2010

Dear Obama,

At the risk of sounding redundant, I want to commend you for being "the most transparent administration in history." We the people, and our respected adversaries, just became privy to the size and scope of the US's nuclear arsenal. Your good offices disclosed that America has just over 5,000 nuclear weapons—5,120 to be exact. In an effort to get other "trustworthy" nuclear nations to be forthcoming, Code Pink came out with the following statement: "We think it is in our national security interest to be as transparent as we can be about the nuclear program of the United States." Actually, that was your Secretary of State Hillary Clinton ... my bad.

It's refreshing to see a President be uber-transparent about our top-secret national security details. Some complain and wish you would be equally transparent with domestic issues such as healthcare and the stimulus bill. Rubbish ... I say screw our enemies. Nuclear secrets is one thing, but I'll be damned if the terrorists, or any other enemy of the state, is made aware of the true cost of Obamacare!

In accordance with your unique version of "shock and awe," it appears that the Pentagon will offer public tours starting early this summer. The highlight for visitors will, of course, be the public viewing of classified material. Officials are limiting access to Monday-Saturday (3 a.m. – 12 p.m.), accepting group appointments for Sundays. Video cameras and copy machines are authorized, but you will have to wear a special wristband.

Opponents of the tours have argued that every despot, dictator, or enemy of the US will take advantage of this unprecedented access. However, proponents anticipated such pushback and have told their critics not to fear. They plan to place a special excise tax on all food and beverage items sold in the cafeteria. Sure our enemies may ultimately get the information they are looking for, but it's definitely going to cost them.

Sincerely,
Chris

P.S. Pre-sold "Twofer" passes have been canceled due to construction at Langley.

May 4, 2010

Dear Obama,

On Saturday, America escaped yet another "man-caused disaster." An SUV, packed with explosives, was abandoned in the middle of Times Square. Fortunately, the bomb never went off, prompting Secretary of Homeland Security Janet Napolitano to once again claim, "The system worked."

Immediately, the Sherlocks in the media reported the suspect as a forty-year-old white male. New York City Mayor, Michael Bloomberg chimed in, saying that the person(s) responsible may have been upset about the recent healthcare bill.

DEAR OBAMA

Yet just a few hours ago authorities confirmed that thirty-year-old Faisal Shahzad was responsible for the failed attack. Early reports confirm that although born in Pakistan, Shahzad (also known as Jim Bob) resides in Mobile, Alabama where he lives in a doublewide. He's also the proud owner of a gun rack, trailer hitch, and a Bible. We're getting conflicting reports, but tea appears to be one of his favorite beverages.

Needless to say, it was another tense moment for a city already on edge. What's most troubling to me is how easily tea-partying rednecks can disguise themselves as young Pakistani men.

Sincerely,
Chris

May 5, 2010 (Cinco de Mayo)

Querido Obama,

Alfredo Frankengringo es un Senador de Estados Unidos.

Sinceramente,
Cristobal

DEAR OBAMA

May 6, 2010

Dear Obama,

"Stock Market Crashes!" That was the headline earlier today. Thankfully the markets stabilized a little and the Dow appears to have recouped some of its earlier losses. The drop of 1,000 points makes today the second worst intraday decline in history. Nobody is sure yet what caused the massive sell off, but some are already speculating.

Fear concerning the financial crisis in Greece and other global markets is believed to be the leading cause. Trader error or a technical glitch has also been rumored. Several traders did report seeing Vice President Biden trip over the main power cord during a surprise visit to the NYSE earlier in the day. Also contributing to the market's sour mood was the fact that traders were finally forced to accept that Treasury Secretary Timothy Geithner was actually Treasury Secretary. Until this point, most believed Geithner worked in the mailroom.

Amidst the day's chaos, Speaker Pelosi added a much-needed dose of clarity regarding our current economic conditions. Her office released the following statement at 2:30 p.m. right about the same time the markets were freefalling: "Today's news shows the US economy is gaining ground as jobless claims drop for the third straight week and quarterly earnings reports from the S&P 500 show the biggest jump in earnings since the S&P began trading in 1988." The timing of such a statement is questionable, but aides close to Pelosi said she hasn't been feeling well. It would also explain why she hasn't been seen lately at the medical plaza's "Tox Tuesday".

Sincerely,
Chris

May 9, 2010

Dear Obama,

Daniel P. Moynihan once said, "The single most exciting thing you encounter in government is competence, because it's so rare." Unfortunately, we still have to suffer the consequences of W's incompetence. I would argue that your tenure thus far has put a moratorium on Moynihan's claim. Case in point, look at how you recently handled the oil spill disaster in the Gulf of Mexico. It only took you nine days to respond to this environmental catastrophe. How you ever kept it less than ten days is beyond me. You're like the Jeff Spicoli of decision- making.

In response to your critics, let me remind them that from day one the experts were saying that it was only a couple thousand barrels of oil a day that were gushing into the ocean. You knew you had plenty of time to fit in a brief vacation, a few photo ops, and 36 holes.

You put W's Katrina response time of four days to shame. How that oilman lives with himself I don't know. You would think he'd feel guilty and embarrassed about being the largest recipient of BP's political contributions over the past twenty years. Wait a minute—my mistake—that was you.

DEAR OBAMA

By the way, have you heard anything about floods or something in Tennessee? I heard through a very unreliable, archaic media source that nearly two-dozen people have died in severe flooding in Nashville. I assumed since you, and the rest of the MSM hadn't said anything about it, it was a hoax. Even if it were true, what do they want from you? I mean come on—it's Nashville.

Now let's say, God forbid, a massive flood of shampoo hit the city of Berkeley (the horror). That would be an entirely different story. The 24/7-news cycle would hit the ground running inundating us with heart-breaking images of disheveled youth covered in jojoba and other foreign substances (i.e. Lever 2000). No doubt you'd be flying over the destruction in less than twenty-four hours, taking the lead on coordinating efforts on the ground with first responders, FEMA, and other emergency agencies. You would be implementing Code Red insuring that all roads were open and accessible so weed distribution trucks could continue their deliveries—any disruption to the city's main commerce would cripple it. Sorry, I can't write anymore. The mere thought of such a disaster is too emotional.

Let's just hope you never get this 3 a.m. call ...

Sincerely,
Chris

DEAR OBAMA

May 13, 2010

Dear Obama,

Most levelheaded Americans agree that Treasury Secretary Timmy Geithner is a financial wizard. Yes, we poke fun at him for being a devoted Miley Cyrus groupie and joke that his mother drops him off at work each morning, but we must never forget that he has all but single-handedly paved America's road to economic recovery.

For as much success as he has had, I feel sorry for him. I have no doubt that he is a workaholic and generally stays at the office well past 3 p.m. So I was pleased to see that he took a break and wrote a few Facebook updates—they showed a lighter, more playful side of him:

10:32 a.m. May 12: "I'm sitting in my office drinking a Caprisun and playing Guidditch. Barack wants the Money Supply report today. I'm thinking of telling him Bo ate it."

11:17 a.m. May 12: "Bernanke keeps calling and bugging me. Rambles on about deficits, Greece, Armageddon, blah…blah…blah. Thinks he's the second coming of Milton Friedman. I'll give him the bald head, but that's it."

11:46 a.m. May 12: "Snuck a whoopi cushion under Biden's seat during a senatorial meeting this morning. He blamed the "commotion" on Feinstein who was sitting next to him. She ran out in tears. Never underestimate the "Bidster.""

DEAR OBAMA

1:07 p.m. May 12: "Accidentally smashed my thumb with a hammer putting up a Justin Bieber poster in my office. The throbbing is killing me. Though it's nothing like the pain I felt when I tore my ACL chasing after Zac Efron's limo."

5:10 p.m. May 12: "SSSSHHHHH... hiding under my desk. I still haven't finished $ supply report. Barack's coming. I set up a Ferris Bueller-like dummy at my desk. Can hear him coming down the hallway. Crossing fingers. son of a . . ."

Sincerely,
Chris

May 20, 2010

Dear Obama,

Mexico's President, Felipe Calderon gave an address yesterday morning denouncing Arizona' new anti-illegal immigration bill. Only in America can a foreign head of state criticize one of our state's laws while standing on the White House lawn.

For his encore performance, Calderon today stood on the House floor and said the following: "I'm convinced comprehensive immigration reform is crucial to securing our border, but I strongly disagree with the recently adopted law in Arizona ... It's a law that not only ignores reality, but also introduces racial profiling as a basis of law enforcement."

DEAR OBAMA

In a stunning act of patriotism, half of the room (Democrats) stood up and gave Calderon a standing ovation. Our dear Eric Holder, Hilary Clinton, and Janet Napolitano proudly applauded from the front row for the world to see. No doubt we'll see Calderon embark on his diva tour later this week with stops on *The Daily Show* and *Chelsea Lately*.

Certainly Vice President Biden, Speaker Pelosi, Senate Majority Leader Reid and others had Mexico's immigration laws in mind when they stood up for human rights. Here's a snippet of the many humanitarian provisions outlined in Mexico's Ley General de Población (General Law of the Population):

- If outsiders do not enhance the country's economic or national interests or are not found to be physically or mentally healthy, they are not welcome.
- The Mexican government will bar foreigners if they upset the equilibrium of the national demographics.
- Illegal entry into the country is equivalent to a felony punishable by two years of imprisonment.
- Document fraud is subject to fine and imprisonment.
- Those seeking to obtain Mexican citizenship must show a birth certificate, provide a bank statement proving economic independence, pass an exam and prove they can provide their own healthcare.

My personal favorite coincidentally mirrors the Arizona bill which Congress denounced, "Law enforcement officials at all levels, by national mandate, must cooperate to enforce immigration laws, including illegal alien arrests and deportations."

Hmm . . . I wonder if Mexico got its ideas from Tancredo?.

Sincerely,
Chris

May 26, 2010

Dear Obama,

Fallout continues regarding Pennsylvania Congressman Joe Sestak. The Right is in a frenzy over the apparent cabinet position you offered him in an effort to get him to drop his primary bid against Arlen Specter. If in fact it is true, that you or one of your senior officials did offer him a position (Secretary of Navy) to drop out of the race, charges and possibly jail time could follow. Thankfully it's basically the same charge as Blagojevich's so you should be squeaky clean. By now you would have thought that the people had finally warmed up to Chicago's "pay to play" style of politics.

Fortunately, you have White House spokesman Robert Gibbs holding down the fort. He's uh . . . been laser sharp in . . . uh, articulating . . . uh . . . uh, the White House's . . . .uh defense.

None of this really comes as any surprise. In 2009, the *Denver Post* reported that your administration offered

Democratic Senate hopeful, Brad Romanoff, a White House position if he dropped his primary bid against Democratic Senator Michael Bennett. This coincides with another report that Iran's leader, Mahmoud Ahmadinejad was also offered a high-ranking federal job if he suspended Iran's nuclear proliferation program.

 Sincerely—wait just a minute—what's this? Here I'm about to sign off for today and there's breaking news that you're going to do a press conference. Say it ain't so—I guess it was only a matter of time—309 days to be exact. With any luck, this "full blown" press conference will quell much of the misguided scrutiny over your competence, leadership, and golf schedule. Anyway, good luck. I've got my fingers crossed that the press won't ask you about skipping out on the Memorial Day service this weekend in order to go on vacation.

You are by far the military's greatest secret admirer . . .

Sincerely,
Chris

May 29, 2010

Dear Obama,

White House officials could not have been more honest and forthright when breaking the much-anticipated Sestak news on the Friday before Memorial Day weekend. According to White House Chief Counsel Bob Bauer, former President

DEAR OBAMA

Clinton was the one who talked to Rep. Joe Sestak about dropping out of the race against Arlen Specter.

At the urging of your White House, Gillooly to be specific, President Clinton asked Sestak if he would abandon his plans of a primary challenge against Specter, in return for a non-paying advisory job (slightly different than the high ranking federal job Sestak mentioned). The communication supposedly took place last summer, which is only six months earlier than the three months that Sestak claimed. What, did Biden put this story together? Just kidding, I mean, it's a perfectly airtight story. By the way, what were the chances that you and Clinton would meet up for lunch yesterday? If only you would have planned ahead, the two of you could have talked about this.

I guess what we can conclude from all of this is that Joe Sestak was going to give up a possible Senate seat in exchange for a non-paying advisory job. What's not to believe about that? Move along people ...

Not to be outdone, Hillary snatched a little of her hubby's limelight today. She was speaking to an audience at the Brookings Institution today when she said the following: "The rich are not paying their fair share in any nation that is facing the kind of employment issues [America currently does]—whether it's individual, corporate or whatever [form of] taxation forms."

She stole my heart ...

Sincerely,
Chris

DEAR OBAMA

P.S. Have a great Memorial Day weekend. Who needs to acknowledge our veterans and falling heroes anyway?

June 3, 2010

Dear Obama,

Unnamed sources witnessed a heated exchange today in the White House cafeteria between Vice President Biden and veteran White House Press Corps member, Helen Thomas (89 years-young). Apparently Biden was irate after Thomas cut in line ahead of him and took the last serving of chicken Marsala. Tempers flared and soon Biden had her in a headlock.

  Thankfully, Congressman John Dingel (83 years-old) quickly grabbed a bowl of Minestrone and threatened to throw it at Biden if he didn't release her. In the end, cooler heads prevailed. The Vice President apologized for the assault and excessive foul language and Thomas said that she was sorry for dropping a scoop of Spimoni ice cream into Biden's coat pocket.

Just another crazy day in Washington . . .

Sincerely,
Chris

DEAR OBAMA

June 8, 2010

Dear Obama,

I see that the DNC is bracing for a bruising mid-term election. Oh thee of little ACORN faith. Where is the optimism? Where is the hope? I do feel sorry for some of these incumbents. Despite your impending "Get Out the (Dead) Vote," 2010 will most likely be the end of the line for some of these fine public servants. You, on the other hand, are looking just fine for 2012. Your inaction on the deficit, the oil spill, jobs, national security, etc. will be a moot point come 2012, particularly if one follows the Mayan Calendar.

This should cheer you up:

Albright: i don't blame the prez 4 being upset
Biden: so u r taking his side?
Albright: of course i am!
Biden: i think u r both being a little over dramatic
Albright: really! u invited the cast of jersey shore 2 stay in the lincoln bedroom
Biden: and?
Albright: u might as well have invited sheen and his entourage
Biden: u can leave charlie out of this!!
Albright: sorry i didn't know u were a fan
Biden: r u kidding! i just bought men at work on blu ray
Albright: nice . . . very underrated

DEAR OBAMA

Biden: i appreciate the 2 cents maddie
Albright: good luck getting O 2 approve the slumber party. i hope the situation doesn't go streaking thru the WH
Biden: he's harmless
Albright: we'll see

Sincerely,
Chris

June 13, 2010

Dear Obama,

What a weekend! My dad, brother, some family friends, and I went on a golf trip up to Mammoth Mountain. We played fifty-four holes in two days. I know this probably sounds like child's play to you these days, but for me it was the most golf I've ever played in a weekend.

It was fun going with our family friends. They have a cabin up there and have been going for years. They know all the history, landmarks, and secrets of Mammoth Mountain. My friend's dad drove us around and gave us our own personal tour
of the area. One bit of information I found interesting was that despite the record snowfall this past winter, "experts" still claim the region is in a severe drought. City officials and other bureaucrats continue raising the drought standards for the "Save the Delta Smelt" campaign. Ever hear of it?

DEAR OBAMA

You remember California congressmen Dennis Cardoza and Jim Costa, don't you? These were the two Democrats you bribed by increasing the central valley water supply for the workers and farmers in their districts, in exchange for a "yes" vote on your healthcare bill. I'm sorry—not bribed—that's too harsh a word. Let's just say these two were "strongly encouraged" to support Obamacare. Regardless of how it played out, I think we're all grateful that the smelt lives. Instead of griping about it, the 80,000 unemployed farmers and workers should be proud of their sacrifice.

I must give you props for pressuring Congress over the weekend for an additional $50 billion in "emergency" stimulus. You said the aid is needed for state and local governments, and that "the money is needed to avoid massive layoffs of teachers, police, and firefighters." We know this push for more stimulus money has nothing to do with your symbiotic relationship with unions, but is solely based on the resounding success of your first stimulus. That initial stimulus for $787 million (actually $840 million when all is said and done) exceeded expectations and unemployment only went up about 40% after it was implemented. The best part was that we taxpayers got to be part of the solution as our tax dollars went towards worthwhile programs and projects that were guaranteed to revive the economy.

Here are just a few examples:

- The NIH gave hundreds of thousands to a Indiana professor for a study on how kids perceive foreign accents

- Several million went towards a "train-horn-free" zone in Tualitan, Oregon
- Arizona State University and the University of Arizona received a million dollars to study ants
- Nearly half a million went to the State University of Buffalo-New York to study young adults who drink malt liquor and smoke weed (researchers claim that "malt liquor consumption is an understudied topic")
- A hundred thousand given to UMass to study pollen from the Viking Age
- A quarter of a million went towards studying why young men do not like condoms
- Thirty thousand went to the University of Maryland to determine if meth is a rat aphrodisiac.

I've been assured that this is not a Woody Allen rhapsody, but rather a disciplined approach to economic recovery that would no doubt inspire the likes of Stiglitz, Laffer, and Friedman.

Sincerely,
Chris

P.S. Sorry to tease you about the golf ...

DEAR OBAMA

June 18, 2010

Dear Obama,

Lakers take the Celtics in seven! Kobe Bryant named Finals MVP! Back to back champs! Ahmadinejad vows to wipe Israel off the map!

Déjà vu all over again ...

Sincerely,
Chris

June 23, 2010

Dear Obama,

Not that I really care, but it's my birthday today. As you can tell, I'm very excited. Honestly, what's there to be so excited about? I'm one year closer to Bingo tournaments and prune juice. Yes, the plaid pants and crankiness is appealing, but the giant sunglasses ... really?

I have no plans today other than to go to work and have a nice family dinner at my favorite Italian restaurant. What else can you do when your birthday is on a Wednesday? I didn't even get to sleep in. So far the highlight of my day is catching a little of the World Cup before work this morning. Not that I'm much of a soccer fan, but I'll watch the World Cup as long as the US is still in it. They're currently playing Algeria for a chance to advance to the next round. As of right now, it's a 0–0 nail biter.

My biggest gripe against soccer is that I never see any live goals. I'll be into a game and will get up for two seconds to grab a drink out of the fridge while the score is 0-0. It never fails, when I come back it's 1–0. I'm convinced that if I were to watch every minute of every game during the World Cup the games would all end in a 0–0 tie.

GOAL!!! We just scored in the 81st minute to take a 1–0 lead over Algeria ... so I heard.

Sincerely,
Chris

"There's been a lot of excitement that's been growing over the last several years and now with partnering with BP we will have the resources to actually carry out some of the things we want to do in order to help save the world."

– Steven Chu, Secretary of Energy (2007-UC Berkeley)

June 25, 2010

Dear Obama,

The people are growing restless. They're starting to question your leadership capabilities because of the Gulf oil spill. What did they expect considering you've never run a lemonade stand. Seriously, come on people. Must we continuously remind people how successful you were with that community thingy?

The plain fact is that your style of leadership is just different. By different, I simply mean you don't do anything. Some leaders take action during a crisis—you take a bogey. It's not rocket science. Unfortunately, this brilliant tactic has not gone over very well with the American people. They foolishly expect tangible results; they have no idea what's going on behind the scenes. As "The Unseen One" you've been intellectually battling the oil spill. Your intelligence and scholarly background have done far more to slow the oil leak than BP's oil cap. Frankly, I'm amazed the leak has gone on as long as it has with your Columbia and Harvard Law Review experience. It's also quite clear that this leak has no idea you're a best-selling author.

As for the people, whom do they want running the show? Do they want a "leader" like Louisiana Governor Bobby Jindal? This maniac has gone rogue and taken matters into his own hands. I still can't believe he just ordered the National Guard to build a barrier wall off the shore of Louisiana. He's completely unhinged. He is hell-bent on keeping the oil from hitting the shores of the state he has sworn to protect. This is exactly the type of cowboy leadership we're tired of. For crying out loud, he didn't even fill out the proper paperwork. Hello ... Mr. Holder?

In any case, America is going to get a taste of what real leadership looks like tonight. Your prime time presidential address will surely justify your stealth reaction to this environmental catastrophe. A golden opportunity may have presented itself for it looks like you're going to use the Gulf oil disaster to push cap and trade legislation. The Climate Bill was dead in the water until now. If I know you as well as I think I do, you will be pulling a page from Gillooly's old playbook, "never let a good crisis ..." well, you know the rest.

Ironically, Senators John Kerry and Joe Lieberman, privately sought BP's advice when they wrote the bill. If passed, BP stands to make a fortune—a sad consequence the oil giant will just have to live with.

Speaking of, is Gillooly still living rent-free in that BP advisor's D.C. apartment?

Sincerely,
Chris

"First things first, when it comes to [Fannie Mae and Freddie Mac], Congress needs to get them reformed, get them streamlined, get them focused, and then I will consider other options."

– President George W. Bush, August 9, 2007

June 29, 2010

Dear Obama,

I have a couple of Political Darwin Award entries to share

with you, but first let me say congratulations on your new parkway. I heard on the new that they just unveiled the Barack Obama Parkway near Orlando. Your first of many I'm sure. Though it's virtually unheard of for a sitting president to receive such an honor (let alone in his first eighteen months), consider this three-mile stretch of roadway as a little token of appreciation for a job ... done.

Now onto two new Darwin contenders ... Yes, the 2010 pool just got a little bigger. Surprise, surprise, both entries are Democrats. I have no idea what it is with our Donkeys these days, but they sure have cornered the market on ridiculous. Pennsylvania's Paul Kanjorski threw his hat in the ring with a beautifully worded rant during a joint House-Senate conference committee session. The seventy-three-year-old Democratic House member expressed his thoughts on a national expansion of a governmental assistance program which helps financially stressed families avoid foreclosure on their homes. He argued that the money was not being wasted on "minorities" or "defective" people or those who had been irresponsible, as he stated, "They are not minorities, and they're not all the things you like to insinuate that these programs are about. These are average, good American people." Not bad for a rookie. I don't know if it will be enough to take it this year, but he definitely has an outside chance.

On the other hand, Peggy West will most certainly be a finalist in this year's contest. West, a Milwaukee County Supervisor, was in a county board meeting when she explained why she did not think it was necessary for Wisconsin to boycott Arizona because of its new immigration law: "I understand why Texas might want to," she explained, "but not Arizona because, [Arizona] is a state that is a ways removed from the border, and it just doesn't make sense to me." She later went on to explain why gravity wasn't necessary, saying, "it just doesn't make sense to me."

As much as I have become a big fan of hers, I feel that her position as a county supervisor is going to hurt her chances of victory. There's no national exposure. She is no doubt talented, but she is still playing in the minor leagues. Plus, she might have to face our first-ever dual entry. You heard me right. I'm currently researching the bylaws and what they say about two people submitted as one entry. I've come across nothing that would invalidate the nomination.

The trailblazers in question are none other than D.C. veterans, Chris Dodd and Barney Frank. The ambiguously brave duo has been working day and night on this so-called financial regulation bill. The current economic crisis finally prompted Congress to fix the system, and who better to address the problem than the two individuals most intimately involved with it?

I also want to recognize other team members for their integral part in "Operation Hoover, Part Deux:" Franklin Raines, Jamie Gorelick, Robert Rubin, Chuck Schumer, and Hank Paulson. Despite the contributions of team "7 to 10ers," Dodd and Frank remain the face of Fannie Mae and Freddie Mac. The two repeatedly assured Congress and the public that Fannie Mae, Freddie Mac, and the economy as a whole were just fine. Or as Barney Frank said in 2002, "I do not regard Fannie Mae and Freddie Mac as problems … I do not think we are facing any kind of a crisis." During the same period, Dodd continued to deny rumors that Fannie and Freddie were in a financial emergency. He called the firms "fundamentally strong" and in "sound situation" and "good shape." He concluded by saying, "to suggest that they are in major trouble is not accurate."

Since the Darwin committee is a stickler for rules, the above-mentioned comments are null and void due to the statute of limitations. However, during a recent press conference, a teary-eyed Dodd, who is the chairman of the Senate Banking Committee, had this to say on behalf of the new Dodd-Frank bill: "No one will know until this is actually in place how it works. But we believe we've done something that has been needed for a long time."

Passing the biggest financial regulatory bill since the Great Depression without knowing how it works (i.e. healthcare) is sure to be worth a golden ticket to this year's main event. Here's to you **F**rank and **D**odd **R**espectively. Hey, what do you know? . . . FDR.

Sincerely,
Chris

P.S. When I first heard of the Dodd/Frank bill I thought it was a measure to personally regulate Chris Dodd and Barney Frank ... my bad.

DEAR OBAMA

June 30, 2010

Dear Obama,

I had trouble sleeping last night and I'm certain it had something to do with yesterday's entry. As soon as I concluded, I realized that I had done a poor job of getting my point across. Let me make it clear—George W. Bush was largely responsible for the Fannie Mae and Freddie Mac disaster. There's no point in analyzing it any further. We know the damage he's done. He walks the streets a free man and there's nothing we can do about it. Power and privilege will always trump justice. That's the way the system works. But hey, don't take it from me; take it from W's own words:

> [Fannie and Freddie] provide liquidity in the mortgage market that benefits millions of homeowners, and it is vital they operate safely and operate soundly. So I've called on Congress to pass legislation that strengthens independent regulation of the GSEs and ensures they focus on their important housing mission. The GSE reform bill passed by the House earlier this year is a good start. But the Senate has not acted. And the United States Senate needs to pass this legislation soon.

How about one more quote, dated May 3, 2008, for good measure:

> Americans are concerned about making their mortgage payments and keeping their homes. Yet Congress has

DEAR OBAMA

failed to pass legislation I have repeatedly requested to modernize the Federal Housing Administration that will help more families stay in their homes, reform Fannie Mae and Freddie Mac to ensure they focus on their housing mission, and allow State housing agencies to issue tax-free bonds to refinance sub-prime loans.

Where's the Grand Jury? . . .

Sincerely,
Chris

"Any health care funding plan that is just, equitable, civilized and humane must redistribute wealth from the richer among us to the poorer and the less fortunate. Excellent health care is by definition redistributional."

– Donald Berwick, Administrator of the Centers for Medicare and Medicaid Services

July 7, 2010

Dear Obama,

Your White House has been very busy these days. Not only did we get the news yesterday that your Justice Department is suing the state of Arizona for enforcing federal immigration law, but also your plan to confirm Donald Berwick as the administrator of the Centers for Medicare and Medicaid Services. It is odd that he had difficulty gaining the support of both Republicans and Democrats. Since a bruising confirmation battle was inevitable, you really had no choice but to bypass the Senate and use the recess appointment.

While Berwick did refer to Britain's National Health Service as "one of the greatest health care institutions in human history" and "a global treasure," it doesn't necessarily mean he intends to turn the American health care system into a carbon copy of Britain's government-run health system. He did go on to say in 2008, "I fell in love with the NHS. To an American observer, the NHS is such a seductress ... Like any lover, it took me a while to see the blemishes of my beloved, though I soon had help from people quite willing to point out the warts." Smeagol (Berwick) also admits to referring to the NHS as "my precious," but emphatically denies harassing anyone named Frodo.

We all know this appointment had nothing to do with his love affair with rationed health care ("The decision is not whether or not we will ration care – the decision is whether we will ration with our eyes open. And right now, we are doing it blindly.") or his disdain of the free market. Like you, Smeagol is all about transparency. Hopefully, Berwick will be able to get the health care system of his dreams, help turn America into a European suburb and convince the public that Gollum is his stepbrother.

With any luck your recent lawsuit might just give Arizona Governor Jan Brewer the prison sentence she deserves. If nothing else, it will put her gross negligence and racism on display for the world to see. Arizona's new

DEAR OBAMA

immigration law is a human rights violation and has no place in an enlightened free society.

I echo the comments Michael Posner (Assistant Secretary of State for Democracy, Human Rights, and Labor) said back in May. During a US-China bilateral human rights dialogue, Posner was asked if they (China and the US) discussed Arizona's new law, to which he responded:

> We brought it up early and often. It was mentioned in the first session and as a troubling trend in our society, and an indication that we have to deal with issues of discrimination or potential discrimination. And these are issues very much being debated in our own society.

Finally! It's about time that the US apologizes to China for our own human rights atrocities. China's been getting a bad rap over the years. I think it's time we take a long hard look in the mirror. We have plenty to apologize for: *Jersey Shore*, Kathy Griffin, the Snuggie . . . At least China now has a solid defense any time it is accused of human rights atrocities, "Hey, at least we're not America."

Sincerely,
Chris

DEAR OBAMA

"Al Qaeda is racist against black members from West Africa because they are only used in lower level operations. In short, Al Qaeda is a racist organization that treats black Africans like cannon fodder and does not value human life."

– White House Official, July 2010

July 14, 2010

Dear Obama,

Results are in—race issues in this country have considerably simmered down over the past two years. You have kept your campaign pledge to be a post-racial president. The media is largely to thank for this; however, you and your operatives deserve some credit as well.

Despite this unprecedented progress we did have a little dustup recently. The NAACP (a political arm of the Democrat party) passed a resolution yesterday condemning "extremist elements" within the Tea Party. "Well, duh." Tell us something we don't know. The group claims that Tea Party members spat on and called Congressman John Lewis and other members of the black caucus derogatory names during Speaker Pelosi's much publicized health care bill procession.

Despite intense scrutiny and a $100,000 reward, no one has come forward to substantiate the accusations. It seems that not a single cell phone or media camera captured the incidence(s).

Regardless, it's still an outrage...

Sincerely,
Chris

July 17, 2010

Dear Obama,

Watchdog group Minnesota Majority reviewed the voting records from Al Franken's 2008 razor-thin senatorial win. It concluded that at least 341 convicted felons voted illegally in two of Minnesota's 87 counties during the 2008 general election. They have yet to review the other 85 counties, but it's probably safe to say this isn't an isolated occurrence. I guess we now know which party attracts the more politically astute felons.

Hence, Al Franken is a United States Senator...

Sincerely,
Chris

July 21, 2010

Dear Obama,

The Bulldog is at it again. Florida Congressman Alan Grayson once again threw down the gauntlet. I've never seen a contender more determined to take the Political Darwin Awards. Late Monday, after most Congressmen had left, Grayson, the millionaire, stood on the House floor before several interns and a janitor and said the following regarding the job crisis and the unemployment bill:

> Now, I know what the Republicans are thinking. They're thinking why don't they just sell some stock. If they're in really dire straits, maybe they could take some of their art collection and send it off to the auctioneer. And if they're in deep, deep trouble maybe these unemployed can sell one of their yachts. And I will say this to the Republicans who have blocked this bill now for months and kept food out of the mouths of children, I will say to them now, may God have mercy on your souls."

If nothing else, Congressman Grayson is wicked smart. His hysteria sealed the deal—he is now the poster child for the Political Darwin Awards! This shouldn't come as a shock to anyone. He comes to the table with impeccable credentials. He's a lawyer, a radical leftist, a congressman, and Harvard educated (B.S. in Hemp).

This contest was over before it even began . . .

Sincerely,
Chris

DEAR OBAMA

July 27, 2010

Dear Obama,

I don't know much about the WWE, but the smackdown you delivered to the Republicans on Monday was fantastic. You finally called them out for their egregious opposition to the Senate campaign finance bill. You called it partisan gamesmanship that threatens to give special interests undue influence on US elections, or in your own words, "You'd think that reducing corporate and even foreign influence over our elections would not be a partisan issue."

One could view this as hypocritical considering you accepted millions of undisclosed online donations, most of which came from unknown sources overseas. In your defense, the totals were only estimated to be in the hundreds of millions, in effect, having no real impact on the '08 election. As long as an independent organization doesn't decide to do a 2008 audit of your presidential campaign donations you should be golden.

By the way, I'm giving up on the Bald Rejuvenation Tour and the entire campaign altogether. In fact, I'm looking into getting a piece. I know this probably means I'm going straight to hell. The support is not there and I just don't have the strength anymore.

I was online the other day and there are so many exciting options and alternatives out there for people like me. For instance, did you know they offer eco-friendly toupees? How cool is that! Not only can alopecia sufferers now rejoin normal society, but they can also reduce their carbon imprint. This exciting new line is made from the shed hair of sustainable boars and recycled broom bristles.

What's also exciting is that I found a company online that specializes in creating hair fantasies. The company got the idea from the old Arnold Schwarzenegger sci-fi flick *Total Recall*. In the movie there was a company called Rekall that implanted false memories of virtual trips into a person's brain. The customer could choose to have any identity he wanted. They could be a spy, a famous actor, a tycoon, etc. The fantasy options were endless.

The hair company I'm researching is waiting for FDA approval on their patented implantable chip. The basic idea is to offer the baldtrodden virtual experiences of having hair. Some of the more popular simulations include revisiting the barber, riding in a convertible, the static balloon experience, and for platinum members, the Bon Jovi "Bang your Head" package. This includes fronting the legendary rock band at New York's Giants Stadium.

Yes, Mr. President, I am a weak man . . .

Sincerely,
Chris

"Obama is the head of the dysfunctional family of America – a rational man running a most irrational nation."

– New York Times Columnist Maureen Dowd, August 2010

DEAR OBAMA

August 3, 2010

Dear Obama,

Question: According to governmental data, under which president did income from private businesses shrink to their smallest portion of personal income in US history while at the same time, government-provided benefits such as social security, unemployment, food stamps, and other programs rose to a record high.

- A. Carter
- B. Hoover
- C. FDR
- D. Obama

Oh, never mind, like you don't know. In any case, let me just say congratulations.

 I am curious to know what the talking heads have to say about this. Their relentless "Socialist this" and "anti-Capitalist that" has been debunked for the umpteenth time. Thankfully, for a man with extra thick skin, lame antagonism like this doesn't bother you. You've never been one to engage in petty bickering or accusatory language. Yes, you've sparred with Rush Limbaugh, Fox News, Israel, the Commerce department, Snooki (taxing tanning salons), etc., but you've done so without diminishing presidential decorum. You're smart enough to realize that behaving like a five-year-old is not becoming for a former-community-organizer-turned-leader-of-the-free-world. All that matters is ideology, transformation, and achieving that stubbornly elusive "worker's paradise." All the rest is just static.

If we're going to be honest here, most of the "isms" they're labeling you with should be worn as a badge of honor. We know they work; it's just a matter of doing them right. The main reason communism was only an above average ideology is because Lenin and Stalin didn't know what the heck they were doing. It was like the capitalist leading the capitalist. Despite their incompetence, they at least got the marketing right. They conveyed the message well but unfortunately it all came down to execution ... sorry, wrong choice of words. It all came down to implementation. Had those wannabe iron-fisters had an Ivy League education, history would be telling a different story today.

It's totally the reverse with your administration. The implementation is good, but the marketing sucks. Some would blame public speaking expert White House Spokesman, Robert Gibbs. This may or may not be true. What I'm trying to say is that you need to rebrand. The humble workaholic image is commendable, but it's not working. You need a slogan— something catchy— something the folks will really take to.

If I were your "Marketing Czar" I would scrap your current advertising campaign and change plain old Marxism and Socialism to "Vitamin Marxism" or "Smart Socialism." Yes, you might run into patent issues, but that's nothing Holder and the rest of the DOJ can't handle. Strategically it makes sense, plus the timing is crucial.

You have a huge fight over the expiration of Bush's tax cuts ahead of you. If the people take to your new cool slogan it will be much easier to convince them that letting the tax cuts expire and taking more money from small businesses and the middle class is a good thing.

Sincerely,
Chris

P.S. Yesterday, ethics charges were handed down against Congresswoman Maxine Waters (D-CA). Congressman Charlie Rangel (D-NY) expressed his disappointment, but said that he's looking forward to carpooling with her to court.

August 11, 2010

Dear Obama,

It's been a while since I've heard any good news, but hearing that the House passed another jobs bill yesterday was music to my ears. In an emergency session, the House passed a $26 billion state and local aid package that will go to help teachers and other state employees.

After discussing the bill with my four-year-old, he concluded that the chances of powerful unions skimming money off the top of this giveaway were as likely as Curious George getting into mischief. I hope he is right and that much of the money from this "job saving" bill will be well spent helping liberal Democrats get elected in November. The fact that taxpayer money will ultimately be going to help elect/reelect the same people that the public is "fed up" (enamored, impressed with, in awe of) with is ironic to say the least.

This just goes to show you how different Congress is from your run-of-the-mill organized crime family. Aside from the thievery, corruption, racketeering, intimidation, and political payoffs, they have nothing in common.

Sincerely,
Chris

August 12, 2010

Dear Obama,

Early on in your tenure I encouraged you to look towards California for guidance and sanity, particularly the Golden State's court system. You may or may not have taken my suggestion seriously, but the recent court decision to overturn Proposition 8 (gay marriage ban) in California should speak for itself.

Justice finally prevailed when the honorable Vaughn Walker nullified the votes of seven million Californians who believe marriage should be between one man and one woman. He based his decision on the premise that a ban on gay marriage violates an individual's basic rights. Precedent was crucial in his decision. He cited excerpts from *Will and Grace* and Perez Hilton's blog. He hoped to reference the Constitution, but ultimately concluded that the Constitution is itself unconstitutional.

Predictably the bigots claim his activism reeks of

tyranny and that it's just one more cultural attack on our Republic. Had Judge Walker been thorough in his research he could have silenced the critics by invoking the 27th amendment. This amendment, as outlined by our Founding Persons, clearly states, "that all people, created in the image of Mother Nature, shall have the inalienable right to engage in any marriage style that suits them." It goes on, "Although the definition of marriage declares it's between one man and one woman, this is purely subjective. If an enlightened judge deems that the phrase "one man and one woman" actually means two men and no woman, or three men and one woman then so be it. These cases shall be valid because there must be no discrimination." Anyway, this little civics lesson should quiet those who question this judge who defied the will of the people and single-handedly redefined marriage.

In any case, Judge Walker put a hold on gay marriages until August 18th. Then it will most likely go to San Francisco's Ninth Circuit Court of Appeals where the case is sure to be reaffirmed. Ultimately, most experts believe the case will end up making it all the way to the Supreme Court. It is probably irrelevant to note that Judge Walker is openly gay, as it clearly had no bearing on his decision. He also happens to be a baby boomer.* Again, it's highly improbable this played any part in his decision. The chances that bong resin affected his clarity or judgment are minimal at best.

Sincerely,
Chris

DEAR OBAMA

*Baby Boomer: An individual whose daily marijuana intake has exceeded their daily fruit, vegetable, and protein consumption and who has accumulated at least 1,000 flight hours from sniffing glue.

August 17, 2010

Dear Obama,

All the media coverage at the moment is about a New York City Imam's plan to build a mosque near Ground Zero. Upon completion, the so-called "Cordova Project" would be a thirteen-story Islamic cultural center 600 feet away from Ground Zero. Much of the feigned outrage is over this Imam Feisal Rauf's "questionable" background. The Right is in a tizzy over a few innocuous comments he has made in the past. Apparently some feel that saying the "US was an accessory to 9/11," or that "Osama Bin Laden was made in the U.S.A.," and "the US has more innocent blood on its hands than Al Qaeda" is worrisome. Oh, I almost forgot, it is also troubled because he won't denounce the terrorist organization Hamas.

For some peculiar reason this has a number of New Yorkers and 9/11 families upset. Perhaps they're still a little sensitive about 9/11. I say you invite the Imam and the 70% of Americans who oppose the construction to the White House for another Beer Summit. The first one was such a stellar success, why not do it again?

Sincerely,
Chris

DEAR OBAMA

August 25, 2010

Dear Obama,

Let me start by saying what an honor it was to take my family vacation at the same time as yours. Just knowing we were simultaneously enjoying a little R & R enhanced my vacation experience. I can't think of anybody who deserves a ten-day vacation to Martha's Vineyard more than you. After all, it's only your 6th vacation this year. I, along with hundreds of others, feel you have certainly earned it. The triumph alone of your highly touted "Recovery Summer" is worth an extended vacation at a $1.7 million Emerald Lake Hills home. So with that being said, all middle/lower class Americans such as I wish to thank you for your humble sensitivity and discretion when choosing your vacation destination.

Despite this "Recovery Summer," I worried about taking my vacation when I saw that jobless claims were continuing to climb, housing and manufacturing data was far worse than expected, and the markets were still extremely volatile. Thankfully, Vice President Biden calmed my concerns over the weekend when he assured us that things are "moving forward" and that more stimulus money would give us "a chance to do something big, man." Whew! What a relief! It is obvious that the rumors of a massive disconnect between D.C. and Main Street have been greatly exaggerated.

DEAR OBAMA

America is truly fortunate to have Shemp as its Number Two . . .

Sincerely,
Chris

August 27, 2010

Dear Obama,

Nothing but silence today from the bloodhounds in the media as you concluded your 48th round of golf (in nineteen month) as President of the United States. I would bet (gentlemen's agreement) that in those nineteen months Phil Mickelson has played more rounds of golf than you, so what's the problem?

On a separate note, I have some exciting news! The company I work for invited all its employees to a local fundraiser for Barbara Boxer. The event is a reception and luncheon with Barbara Boxer and special guest Vice President Joe Biden—how awesome is that! Babs and Shemp killin' it in the O.C. The mere thought of sharing the same room with these two academics is rather intimidating, let alone hearing them speak. I might need an intellectual Sherpa to help guide me through the night. I was so excited when I read the itinerary of events.

Here's a sneak peak at the schedule:

    4:00 – 5:00   Cocktails: Open bar

DEAR OBAMA

5:00 – 6:00	Music: Tribute band, "REO Speed-dialer"
6:00 – 7:00	Catered Dinner: Surprise
7:00 – 8:00	Dessert: Jill Biden's famous snickerdoodles
8:00 – 9:00	Auction: Donated items*
9:00 – 10:00	Entertainment: Joe Biden's "Mindfreak," and Boxer's ventriloquist act.

*Donated items include Senator Boxer's macramé plant hangers and seashell bracelets, an autographed picture of Boxer with Zsa Zsa Gabor, and seven of Vice President Biden's vintage polyester leisure suits.

I haven't yet decided if I'm going to pay the minimum $500 donation to attend, but right now I'm struggling to find a reason not to . . .

Sincerely,
Chris

August 29, 2010

Dear Obama,

I wasn't planning to comment on Glen Beck's "Restoring Honor" rally held yesterday, but I can't resist. It really bothers me that so many sheeple attended this charlatan's rally. Thankfully, those of us with a marble still left in our heads did not attend his "rally of hate." We all saw through his charade. Truth is a stubborn thing. It's a shame a few gullible people cannot see him for the fascist that he is.

I was relieved to see many in the MSM mock Beck's attempt to inflate the number of attendees. He claims it was somewhere between 300,000 to 600,000 people. Yet, most Lincoln Memorial crowd attendance experts from Berkeley say the number is really around 80,000 to 100,000. Regardless of how many people participated, there's like 300 million people in the US. So we're only talking about .0003% of the population. Impressive indeed Mr. Beck ...

Look, do I care what the real number is? No. What I really care about are the *hundreds* who were duped into hearing about God. Proselytizing in the public square is an affront to all decent people and Mr. Beck needs to be held accountable. This is exactly why Separation of Church and State is so critical to our thriving nation. Huge strides have been made in this area, and it would be a total shame to lose the momentum to this Bible thumper. The anti-Christian movement has done a great job in convincing us that the founders of this country didn't believe in God and that Divine Providence is a "Gentleman's Club" in West Hollywood.

The Left often sites the writings of "deists," Thomas Jefferson and Benjamin Franklin as proof of our secular heritage. After reading much of their writings, how could one not come to this very conclusion? As Jefferson said in *The Writings of Thomas Jefferson*, page 385:

> God who gave us life gave us liberty. And can the liberties of a nation be thought secure when we have removed their only firm basis, a conviction in the minds

of the people that these liberties are of the Gift of God? That they are not to be violated but with His wrath? Indeed, I tremble for my country when I reflect that God is just; that His justice cannot sleep forever; I am a real Christian – that is to say, a disciple of the doctrines of Jesus Christ.

In case you need a little more convincing, this is written on the Jefferson Memorial:

God who gave us life gave us liberty. Can the liberties of a nation be secure when we have removed a conviction that these liberties are the gift of God? Indeed I tremble for my country when I reflect that God is just, that His justice cannot sleep forever.

In a letter to Ezra Stiles (the President of Yale University) Jefferson's pagan colleague, Benjamin Franklin wrote, "Here is my Creed. I believe in one God, the Creator of the Universe. That He governs it by His Providence. That He ought to be worshipped."

Evidence of Franklin's doubts about God extends beyond fancy quotes and declarations. His actions cemented his skepticism. He was one of the main proponents of the establishment of a paid chaplain in Congress. He chose a New Testament verse for the motto of the Philadelphia Hospital. He proposed a Biblical inscription for the Seal of the United States, and lastly his educational plan for public schools in Pennsylvania insisted that schools teach "the necessity of a public religion and the excellency of the Christian religion above all others, ancient or modern."

I believe these great men would be proud to see how far we've come in eliminating God from our society. Today's culture proves that the relentless attacks on God in schools (prayer and the Pledge of Allegiance), government, courthouses, cemeteries, currency, marriage, and just about every other aspect of our lives has certainly kept America's moral compass strong.

Sincerely,
Chris

P.S. MSNBC host Ed Shultz, of the Ed Shultz Show, was not impressed with Beck's turnout. He "guaranteed" he could bring out 300,000 people or more to hear him speak. A feat I have no doubt he could accomplish, if only people knew who Ed Shultz was . . .

> "Workers of the world unite ... it's not just a slogan anymore."
>
> – Andy Stern, former cadre leader of the SEIU

September 6, 2010

Dear Obama,

Anyone who can get through Labor Day without shedding a tear must be void of emotion, or else they're some kind of bourgeois apologist. As for me, I've been a slobbering fool all day, crying tears of joy and hope for a better day for my worker children and future worker grandchildren.

I was inspired seeing you back with your union peeps at the labor festival today in Milwaukee. Your energy and feistiness sure fired them up. You could just tell they were itching to get back out onto the streets. Their devotion and allegiance to you is ferocious, albeit beautiful.

Unfortunately, union patriarchs Andy Stern and Richard Trumka missed the festivities. As the two most recognizable patriotic intimidators within the labor movement, there is no question that their presence would have brought the house down. Yes, they were missed, but we all understand that they are both very busy individuals these days.

Sterny is doing a heck of a job for you as a member of the White House's National Commission on Fiscal Responsibility and Reform. His tireless devotion to this wildly successful department has some wondering where on earth he found the time to participate in the new reality show, *The Real Biggest Loser.*

The other half of this dynamic duo is former AFL-CIO President, Richard Trumka. El Presidente used to work behind the scenes until someone finally realized that he and his mustache were better suited for the camera. Mr. Trumka is now everywhere promoting your truthaganda at speaking engagements, in op-ed's for *Pravda*, and on the different cable news shows. He made waves a couple of days ago during a speech in Anchorage, Alaska where he warned former Governor Sarah Palin that if she continued her rhetoric, "Palinism" and "McCarthyism" would soon be synonymous.

Although Mr. Trumka doesn't have Andy Stern's panache, his now famous keg stands have rallied supporters at numerous union events. This is quite an impressive feat considering his bulky frame. He's definitely a man's man with the size and strength to take out the kneecap of any non-union member with one swing. However, those closest to him say he is the sweetest teddy bear around.

It just wouldn't feel right if I didn't conclude my Labor Day entry with a passage from the *Good Book**:

> Owing to the extensive use of machinery, and to the division of labour, the work of the proletarians has lost all individual character, and, consequently, all charm for the workman. He becomes an appendage of the machine, and it is only the most simple, most monotonous, and most easily acquired knack, that is required of him.

Word…

Sincerely,
Chris

*Marx, K., and Engels, F. Communist Manifesto. Moscow, Progress Publisher, 1969.

DEAR OBAMA

September 10, 2010

Dear Obama,

Why are members of your administration team abandoning ship? Just when I felt like you all were starting to get your groove on. Former members of your economic team, Christina Romer and Peter Orszag have already left. Now it looks like Gillooly will most likely step down as your Chief of Staff for a chance at his dream job, mayor of Chicago. Since Mayor Daley is not seeking reelection, Gillooly's departure is all but certain.

Having already lost these talented team members, I'm starting to get nervous that Treasury Secretary Timmy Geithner will desert you as well. I'm afraid he may be at a point where he wants to focus full-time on his new creative endeavor. Over the last few months he's been privately pumping his blog "WhatWouldBieberDo?" His blog reminds me of movie critic, Michael Medved's nationally syndicated talk show, which is a unique blend of politics and pop culture (mainly movies). Timmy appears to be following a similar format. Just yesterday, he noted that your new $50 billion "tax cut" stimulus bill was "dope," while also giving *Hot Tub Time Machine* two thumbs up.

Sincerely,
Chris

DEAR OBAMA

September 14, 2010

Dear Obama,

Legolas, son of Thranduil, King of the Woodland Realm, and host of HBO's *Real Time with Bill Maher*, was on Jay Leno last night. Leno asked him about the Ground Zero mosque controversy. As expected, the self-avowed atheist took the opportunity to give a four-minute tirade mocking houses of worship and faith in general.

I affirm the outspoken "Elfin King" for his candor. It's not often you find someone with the courage to take on the religious establishment in this country. He pulled no punches when he described faith as a fairy tale, delusional, and full of mythical figures (much like his own life in the Woodland Realm). His theological knowledge is extraordinary, not to mention the amount of time he spends smoking pot (he was valedictorian of his graduating class at Ridgemont High).

On another note, I have to give props to White House "Science Czar" and proponent of compulsory abortions and sterilization, John Holdren. He was in Oslo last week for a science forum. While discussing the topic of climate change, he captivated his fellow panelists with the following:

> I think one of the failures of the scientific community was in embracing the term global warming. The term global warming is a dangerous misnomer that should be replaced with 'global climate disruption.' ... The term global warming makes the cause easy to ridicule

whenever there is a snowstorm."

He also added that the cause is easy to ridicule once you think about it...

Sincerely,
Chris

Correction: Mr. Legolas no longer resides in the Woodland Realm. Apparently, he recently purchased a 3-bedroom 2-½-bath condo in the Soho District of Helm's Deep.

"What is more important is to find means by which we can redistribute our economic gains to the benefit of all; this is the government's obligation."

– Barack Hussein Obama, Sr.

September 16, 2010

Dear Obama,

A pointless new report came out today disclosing that the US poverty rate is at 14.3%. In other words, one in seven people in the United States is living in poverty. This is the highest percentage in decades. Piggybacking this report was another one, which confirmed that more Americans are on food stamps now than at any other time in history. Working on a hunch, CBS, NBC, and ABC immediately sent out several teams of investigative reporters to Wasilla, Alaska to find the main culprit behind these worrisome numbers.

I firmly disagree that this has anything to do with the policies of your administration, or the Democrats in general. Yes, Democrats have controlled the House, the Senate and the White House these past two years, but they're the champions of the poor ... just ask them.

Yet predictably, the Right has wasted no time jumping all over these figures. Somehow, they feel as though the buck stops with you, Mr. Commander in Chief. Between their outrage and hysteria you would think the country is headed towards a run on Obamavilles. Big deal, so what if we are? I guarantee if they did start popping up they would be the coolest, hippest places to live.

These reports are just one more reason why we need to start reining in Wall Street and corporate executives. There is so much excess in their greedy coffers that siphoning a billion here or a trillion there would be a huge step towards solving the problem. Unfortunately, we all know that the Republicans/Wall Street crooks would do everything in their power to protect their special-interest sugar daddies. Charles Gasparino's new book *Bought and Paid For* highlights this political connection between Washington and Wall Street. As one example: from January 2007 to January 2010 Wall Street firms and executives donated $13.9 *million* dollars to Republicans, while during the same period only donating $20 million to Democrats.

DEAR OBAMA

Hello? . . .

Sincerely,
Chris

September 20, 2010

Dear Obama,

A week or two ago I wrote about union globalization man, Richard Trumka. His ears must have been burning because he just gave a passionate speech to supporters in Columbus, Ohio. The highlight of the speech came when he accused Republicans of "economic treason," an indisputable charge that was met with great fanfare. The stinging indictment of the GOP was par for the course during his lengthy dictatorial address. He threw other pieces of red meat to the crowd, but none was more memorable than this rabble-rousing accusation.

One cannot deny the fact that he has become a rock star over this past year. It's too bad that people are only now getting to know him because his story, both professionally and personally, is truly inspiring. For instance, I'm sure many folks out there would be heartbroken to find out that Mr. Trumka is a long-time sufferer of acute freemarketitis. He was diagnosed several years ago while employed as an errand boy for Ted Turner. Sadly, aside from getting a real job in the private sector, there are no other known treatments. Having been dealt a tough hand, he has never allowed freemarketitis to get in the way of his true purpose in life, bellyaching against "the man." Seeing that his new rock star status was taking its toll, Mr. Trumka's doctors encouraged him to get treatment for the disease. Taking their advice, he became an entrepreneur and started his new line of cologne. Bacon Fat for Men will be on shelves by early 2011.

Sincerely,
Chris

September 24, 2010

Dear Obama,

I haven't decided yet if Delaware's Democratic candidate for Senator, Chris Coons, is my new hero, or my long-lost ideological soul mate. Around twenty years ago, Mr. Coons wrote a piece for Amherst College titled, "Chris Coons: The Making of a Bearded Marxist." The media of course are ignoring this, instead focusing on his opponent's cuticle hygiene. I can understand the media not wanting to waste their time delving into a story as American as apple pie. Unfortunately, he has succumbed to the pressures of Fox News and has said that it was only a joke. It was a convincing statement, but his appearance suggests otherwise. Now balding, he has that pale, beady-eyed, worker-like glow, complimented by a socio-economic swagger only the oppressed could love.

    I don't know if he's confused or just playing the game, but I'm pulling for the guy who once wrote: "I realize that

DEAR OBAMA

Kenya and America are very different, but experiences like this warned me that my own favorite beliefs in the miracles of free enterprise and the boundless opportunities to be had in America might be largely untrue." He also wrote, "Kenya provided a needed catalyst ... I studied under a bright and eloquent Marxist professor at the University of Nairobi ..." Why would he call any of this a joke? I just wish someone would tell him that this is now in vogue—Marxism is the new blue jeans.

Fortunately, he's polling about 15 points higher than his opponent, Tea Party backed candidate, Christine O'Donnell. She is someone who made a name for herself years ago on Legolas' old show *Politically Incorrect*. Normally, I would mock, defame and discredit her, but between cable news, the MSM, late-night shows, blogs, magazines, HGTV, Ukrainian News Agency, Ukrayins'ke Novyny and *Sesame Street* there's nothing you haven't already heard.

Sincerely,
Chris

October 1, 2010

Dear Obama,

White House officials confirmed today that Gillooly is leaving his post as Chief of Staff to run for mayor of Chicago. As I said a few weeks ago, this was a foregone conclusion. I hear Joy Behar is interested in the position.

We all know such departures are common within every administration. People come and go as if there were some sort of political turnstile in Washington. However, your team members are dropping in record numbers—unusual even by D.C. standards.

Regardless of how the Right spins it, America was fortunate to have had these talented and crafty folks serving in your administration, if only for a short time. I bid farewell and best wishes to comrades Peter Orszag, Christina Romer, and Larry Summers (basically your entire economic team). Their successful implementation of the Zimbabwean economic model certainly earns them an early retirement.

David "Diggler" Axelrod and the "Word-Doctor" Robert Gibbs have stated that they intend to leave after the midterms. Secretary of Defense Robert Gates also confirmed his plans to step down in 2011. Assuming it was mandatory, Vice President Biden was packing his suitcase until several aides assured him that he didn't have to leave if he didn't want to.

With so many vacancies in the White House, I must strongly encourage you to appoint (i.e. recess) Florida Congressman Alan Grayson to your administration. Recent polls show him trailing in nearly double digits behind his opponent. This would be a tough loss. Despite my concerns, I haven't completely given up hope. In fact, I'm encouraged by a newly released positive ad. In short, Grayson's ad labels his Republican challenger, Daniel Webster as, "Taliban Dan." It features a short clip of Webster saying, "Wives, submit yourself to your own husband." This is followed by repeated clips of Webster saying, "She should submit to me."

It's a highly effective ad that clearly shows Webster as one of those crazy fundamentalists. The clips were taken from a speech Webster gave at a conference for the nonprofit Christian group, the Institute in Basic Life Principles. This was only an excerpt of his talk. Other excerpts such as: "Don't pick the ones [Bible verses] that say, 'She should submit to me,' rather, pick the ones that you're supposed to do. So instead, you should 'Love your wife even as Christ loved the church and gave himself for it.'" were considered boring and not jazzy enough for the ad. Anyway, the prospect of Grayson not serving the public in some capacity is a crime in and of itself. Please, do America and me a favor by considering his resume if the ad doesn't work and he does indeed lose his job.

Sincerely,
Chris

> *"Theoretically, there is nothing that can stop the government from taxing 100% of income so long as the people get benefits from the government commensurate with their income which is taxed."*
>
> *– Barack Hussein Obama, Sr.*

DEAR OBAMA

October 4, 2010

Dear Obama,

Red, white, and blue is all I can say to describe this past weekend. The "10-2-10" or "One Nation" rally was held this past Saturday at the Lincoln Memorial. Organizers meant it as a response to Glenn Beck's "Restoring Honor" rally, but it was so much more than that. It showed the world that Beck and the conservatives don't have the monopoly on traditional, patriotic American values. Here is a partial list of the organizations that sponsored, supported, and participated in this "family values" gathering (Not included are 400 other special interest groups):

Code Pink, ACLU, Planned Parenthood, Ex-offenders Association of PA, Humanist Party-New York City Chapter, Detroit Democratic Socialists of America, Demand Equity Now, Committee of Correspondent for Democracy and Socialism, Institute of Caribbean Studies (sure, why not?), *Chicago Democratic Socialist of America, National Council of La Raza, New York City Democratic Socialists of America, Climate Crisis Coalition, Welfare Rights Committee, International Socialist Organization, and the Communist Party USA (CPUSA).*

Hate and vitriol were noticeably absent from the event. Amiable signs such as "Glenn Beck and Sarah Palin are racist," "Death thanks the G.O.P for its stance on health care reform," "End all U.$. aid to the racist state of Israel"

DEAR OBAMA

and "The Enemies of America," are just a few examples of the beautiful sentiment which permeated this love-fest. The rhetoric was equally benign with speakers vying for that elusive MLK moment. MSNBC's Ed Shultz kicked things off with, "The conservative voices of America, they are holding you down, they don't believe in your freedom. They want the concentration of wealth. They've shipped your job overseas. . . They suppress your vote." His words of wisdom were well-received; however it was his blue flame specials which won the crowd over. Also addressing the politically active mob was famous-for-something Harry Belafonte. His "I have a dream" moment came when he said the "insidious Tea Party is perilously close to achieving villainous ends." With all due respect, Mr. Belafonte, it's quite clear they've already achieved this goal.

    There was indeed a stark difference between the rallies. Video footage does not lie. The "Restoring Honor" attendees came with their hate, class warfare, racism, and disrespect for the hallowed grounds on which they stood. They may not have left a single piece of trash behind, but their presence alone defiled the Lincoln Memorial. Conversely, the "One Nation" rally brought love, peace, wisdom and respect. Simply disregard the fact that after the rally the grounds of the Lincoln Memorial resembled Timmy Geithner's parents' house after the kegger he had while they were in Europe.

Sincerely,
Chris

DEAR OBAMA

October 7, 2010

Dear Obama,

Austan Goolsbee.

Sorry,
Chris

October 8, 2010

Dear Obama,

Please accept my sincere apologies regarding yesterday's entry. After I read the name Goolsbee, I just couldn't continue. I later regrouped and confirmed it with Snopes. And yes, his name is indeed Austan Dean Goolsbee. It seemed too perfect, too made up...

Anyway, The Treasury Department is now investigating Austan Goolsbee, Chairman of the Council of Economic Advisors. He was allegedly snooping around the tax status of Koch Industries, a corporation privately owned and managed by conservatives. The coincidence, which doesn't exist, is that billionaire brothers Charles and David Koch have given substantially to conservative and Tea Party candidates and causes.

Goolsbee, who denies any relation to the Addams Family, claimed Koch Industries hadn't paid corporate taxes. It was an interesting charge considering it is not a public corporation and its tax disclosures are supposed to remain private. Goolsbee made the unsubstantiated claim while serving on your Economic Recovery Advisory Board. Officials have since said that Goolsbee "won't be making that same mistake again," and that "Morticia might be a third cousin."

It sure would be nice if Mr. Goolsbee could hone his investigative talents and do something about these stagnant job numbers. The word on the street is that he's another one of these young, brilliant, economic prodigies. If only he had a patented formula that would help rev up the economy and start stimulating job growth. We remain stuck at a 9-½% unemployment rate (released earlier today). In fairness, the numbers weren't all that bad. Another report came out today that said $22 million of stimulus money was accidentally sent to inmates and the deceased. The government mailed checks worth $250 each to 72,000 dead people. $250 is certainly reasonable, but with inflation and the cost of staying dead these days, who's to say the extra income will even help?

Our tax dollars also funded a federal study by the National Institute on Alcohol and Alcoholism. The study of "Alcohol and Bar Violence" concluded that bar fights tend to occur in venues that are relatively dark, dirty, noisy, hot, crowded and frequented by a clientele of younger, less agreeable, less conscientious, more impulsive heavy drinkers. Nearly a million dollars for this Einstein study.

Adding some perspective to today's jobs numbers and unemployment rate was Speaker Pelosi: "If you want to create jobs, the quickest way to do it is to provide more funding for food stamps and have unemployment insurance for people who have lost their jobs."

DEAR OBAMA

In case you forgot, she's third in line for the Presidency ...

Biden is number two ...

Cheers,
Chris

P.S. One of your earliest achievements as President was the signing the Homeless Initiative. A recent study shows that homelessness is up a mere 50% over the past year in New York City. This just goes to show you that you can solve any problem if you just throw money at it.

October 14, 2010

Dear Obama,

Not that you've ever worked in an office before, but do you know what really annoys me—co-workers reheating fish in the cafeteria microwave. The stench is unbearable. Office terrorism is what it is. I can see Biden doing something like this in the White House cafeteria. Then again, I can see Jill sending him off each morning with a ham and cheese sandwich, carrot sticks, and gummy-vites. And with all of those fabulous seafood restaurants up north, I bet those Boston boys Sen. John Kerry and Rep. Barney Frank have been guilty of this a time or two.

Speaking of Mr. Frank, how about that free 2009 trip he took to the Virgin Islands? He flew on the private jet of

DEAR OBAMA

Maine Congresswoman, Chellie Pingree's (D-MA) billionaire fiancé, Donald Sussman. At the heart of the story is Paloma Securities, a subsidiary of Sussman's Greenwich, Connecticut based hedge fund. It received $200 million in 2009 as part of the $180 billion federal bailout—next story please.

Obviously the MSM had better things to worry than Frank's innocent excursion. A shocking new photo was revealed of his Republican challenger in the upcoming midterm, Sean Bielat. The photo clearly exposes the thirty-five-year-old's uneven sideburns. This bombshell image has been plastered all over the MSM, the internet, and cable news. Fortunately for Congressman Frank, it couldn't have come at a better time, because until now the fifteen-term House Member has been in the biggest fight of his political life. Apparently, rumors are swirling that Mr. Bielat recently switched from traditional razors to electric. It's turning out to be a costly decision that has shattered any hopes he had of replacing the eternal Congressman.

Sincerely,
Chris

"We've got shovel-ready projects all across the country that governors and mayors are pleading to fund. And the minute we can get those investments to the state level, jobs are going to be created."

– President-Elect Obama, December 2008

DEAR OBAMA

"We want to get shovel ready projects as quickly as possible that at a minimum significantly enhance ridership and take people off the highways."

– Vice President Joe Biden, June 2009

"There's no such thing as shovel-ready projects."

– President Obama, October 13, 2010

October 16, 2010

Dear Obama,

I think I've mentioned this to you before, but in case I haven't, I'm not a great flyer. I wouldn't go as far as to say I'm afraid of flying, I'm just afraid of crashing. Occasionally, I have to fly for work and this week it's off to Portland, Oregon. I'm flying Alaska Air (not by choice). I made my reservation with American Airlines, forgetting its alliance with Alaska Airlines. The problem, which I don't have to tell you, is that I'm boycotting all things Alaskan because of Her. The scary part is I peeked into the cockpit as I boarded and saw that the co-pilot is a woman. Normally, I wouldn't have an issue with a female pilot, but when you put Alaska and a woman together—disaster is inevitable. Do I think I'm in for one hell of a scary flight … you betcha!

The only saving grace is that the pilot is gray and bald (one of the few times baldness is a welcomed sight).

DEAR OBAMA

Thankfully my seating assignment is better than usual—I'm sitting in a window seat with no one in the middle. At least I won't have to deal with a mom with a screaming baby or a character from *Deliverance* sitting next to me.

I spoke too soon ... I'm pretty certain a terrorist is currently on board our plane, an eco-terrorist to be specific. A twenty-something-year-old male wearing sandals with socks and reeking of muesli just walked passed me. I couldn't help but notice the Rastafarian satchel slung over his shoulder. I'm sure the bag only contains Cornnuts, a hackeysack, and gravel, right?

What are the chances he's one of those environmental extremists who are into blowing up Hummers, SUVs, and power supply plants? Don't get me wrong; I'm 100% for militant environmentalism, particularly when I'm not part of the collateral damage. Although I have to admit blowing up this plane would send a huge message. Planes are one the biggest polluters and consumers of big oil in the world. I sure wish they would come out with an electric plane, or at least a battery operated one. How hard can it be?

Despite the cards being stacked clearly against us, we managed to arrive safely. The successful arrival leads me to believe that the co-pilot has no Alaskan affiliation whatsoever. I didn't hear a peep from Muesli the entire flight. In fact I don't see him anywhere. Did I just imagine him?

Where in the heck? ...

Sincerely,
Chris

DEAR OBAMA

October 23, 2010

Dear Obama,

With the midterms only eleven days away, it's no wonder you've ditched the governing in favor of a full-court press of campaigning. Many grumble that the country has been without a leader for the last two months since you are spending 24/7 on the campaign trail. Yes, a vacant oval office raises some eyebrows considering the state of the economy, but two recent appointments leave me feeling confident that you haven't forgotten about your duties back at 1600 Pennsylvania Ave.

Critics need to look no further than the appointment of Tom Donilon to National Security Advisor. Bringing a former top official at Fannie Mae and lobbyist for Goldman Sachs on board should be proof positive that you're still on you're A-game. According to *Judicial Watch*, Mr. Donilon has zero national security experience, though he was co-captain of his laser tag team.

You praised him in a 2005 *Washington Post* article saying Mr. Donilon has a "wealth" of experience helping to run Fannie Mae. As a top official, he was in charge of "managing" government oversight of the two government-sponsored enterprises, or sponsoring government enterprises of "managing" government. In either case, his bureaucratic background should be met in Washington with open arms.

Despite his success with Fannie Mae, some are still not impressed with his record. According to Bob Woodward's book *Obama Wars,* Secretary of Defense Robert Gates told a few of his associates that Donilon's appointment to the NSC would be a "disaster." It should be noted that Gates, the former Director of Central Intelligence, was just being a punk when he said that.

As feisty as some were over the appointment of Donilon, no one in their right mind could disagree with your appointment of Thomas Nides as Deputy Secretary of State. The former consultant for Citi and Goldman Sachs spent much of last year earning $8 million in salary and bonuses as a Wall St. bank executive (his bank received a federal bailout). He claims that he is still eligible for additional bonus money from Morgan Stanley, another bailout recipient. Call me crazy, but my crystal ball is telling me that both Mr. Donilon and Mr. Nides are well on their way to "Czardom."

Sincerely,
Chris

October 25, 2010

Dear Obama,

Al Franken is a United States Senator.

Sincerely,
Chris

P.S. Seriously . . . Al Franken is a United States Senator.

DEAR OBAMA

November 2, 2010

Dear Obama,

Election Day! I'm so excited I can hardly sit still. I have nothing to report right now except that we received a robocall from Susan Sarandon urging us to vote yes on Prop 19 (legalization of marijuana). It's hard to believe that with her flourishing acting career she could find time in her day to campaign for weed. Was she Thelma or Louise? I can never remember …

Regardless of the political environment, I'm still very excited. I know everyone and their mother is saying the Democrats are in for a bruising. I'm sorry, but I don't believe it for a second. I wholeheartedly agree with what the leaders of the Democrat party are saying. Chairman of the Democratic Congressional Campaign, Chris Van Hollen recently said, "We've won 55 seats over the last two cycles, and we hold virtually every swing seat in the country. That's what makes it a very challenging cycle, but that being said, we will win the majority."

A couple of months ago at a DNC meeting in St. Louis, Vice President Biden was equally confident, "There will be a Democratic majority in the House and a Democratic majority in the Senate. That will be the case. And if it were not illegal, I'd make book on it." He later added, "We're also going to see Democratic governors coming back in a way no one expects."

Rounding out the optimism was Speaker Pelosi. She told ABC's *This Week*: "I'm not nervous at all about Democrats' prospects in November." She continued, "Her party is very proud of its legislative record."

Let me close by saying, win, lose or draw your accomplishments the past two years have been nothing short of remarkable. Due to several stimulus bills, Obamacare, an army of creepy "Czars" and tax cheats, the Beer Summit, and lowering your handicap, America's future has never looked more promising.

Two years ago you spoke of transforming America. At the time I wasn't quite sure what you had in mind, or how you'd go about it. Now transformed through collectivism and MSNBC, I completely understand what you meant. Unfortunately, the Right excoriated you and your ambitious goal. To discourage any success they smeared your reputation, spread lies about you, and undermined you every step of the way. Well, in just a few short hours, the American people are going to give those Republicans a butt-whooping of the likes we've never seen.

Good luck Mr. President ...

Signing off ...

Sincerely,
Chris

November 3, 2010 (Midnight)

Biden: u awake maddie??
Albright: unfortunately
Biden: can u believe this sh**!

DEAR OBAMA

Albright: i guess the politicos were right
Biden: i don't get the american people
Albright: me neither
Biden: they r very heckyl and jeckyl
Albright: jeckyl and hyde?
Biden: all of em
Albright: i'm really sorry joe
Biden: it's not all bad
Albright: how so?
Biden: i may have figured out a way 2 make $26,843 a week
Albright: from home?
Biden: how'd u know?
Albright: turn the t.v. off jb…it's late
Biden: it is off
Albright: joe
Biden: what ?
Albright: remember the pyramid scheme?
Biden: this is different
Albright: get some rest joe
Biden: u r right, big night tomorrow
Albright: i thought the state dinner was friday?
Biden: it is, peter frampton is playing at the community center tomorrow
Albright: i gotta go joe
Biden: ok
Albright: tell the prez i'm sorry about the results
Biden: i knew it would all go 2 hell once simon left idol

DEAR OBAMA

"A government big enough to give you everything you want is strong enough to take away everything you have."

– Thomas Jefferson